THE ULTIMATE CLASSIC CAR QUIZ BOOK

2

The questions, the answers, the stories ...

THE ULTIMATE CLASSIC CAR QUIZ BOOK

2

The questions, the answers, the stories ...

DAVID MILLOY
RUSSELL WALLIS

Copyright © David Milloy, 2021

David M. Milloy has asserted his rights under the Copyright, Designs and Patents Act 1988
to be identified as the author of this work.
All trademarks referred to within the pages of this book are the property of their respective owners. Without limiting the rights under copyright reserved above, no part of this publication may be reproduced, stored in or introduced into a retrieval system, or transmitted in any form or by any means (electronic, mechanical, photocopying, recording or otherwise),
without the prior written permission of both the copyright holder
and the above publisher of this book

Cover, Illustrations and typeset design by
Russell Wallis
RJW|Creative Design,
www.rjwcreativedesign.co.uk
Twitter: @Russelljwallis

Printed by Amazon

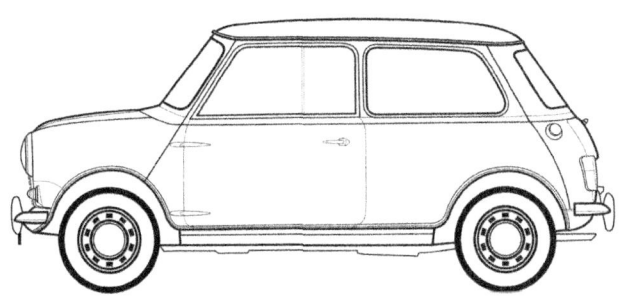

CONTENTS

Introduction ix

About the book x

PART 1
The Questions 1

CATEGORIES

1 General Knowledge 1	2
2 Film & TV	6
3 Numbers Game	10
4 General Knowledge 2	14
5 Motorsport	18
6 It Pays To Advertise	22
7 General Knowledge 3	26
8 The People	30
9 Prototypes & Concepts	34
10 General Knowledge 4	38
11 Lesser Spotted Classics	42
12 United States Of America	46
13 First & Last	50

PART 2
The Answers 55

PART 3
The Stories behind the answers 63

About the authors 176
Also by the same author 177

INTRODUCTION

This is the fourth book (fifth if you count *The Lost Highway*) I've written in the last 18 months. None of them would have existed without the help and support of some fine people, to all of whom I'm very grateful. In particular, my thanks go to Angela, James, Russell, Marcus, Simon, Jonathan, Catherine, Iain and Mike.

My thanks are also gladly given to everyone who has bought one of my books, not least because by buying a book you have enabled me to make donations to over twenty different charities. That matters. A lot.

A quarter of the royalties received from sales of this book will go to charity, and that will continue to be the case with every book I write until (gulp!) people stop buying them. Details of the charities that have benefited will be posted from time to time on my website: www.thelosthighway.online.

The words in this book are mine but the formatting of it and the images that adorn its cover are the work of Russell J. Wallis, a hugely gifted illustrator and thoroughly nice bloke. You can read more about Russell in the 'About the authors' section but suffice it for now to say that, like the A-Team, you can hire him. And you should.

And that's pretty much it. Thank you for purchasing this book. I hope that you enjoy it.

Oh, and one more thing: the obligatory word or two about copyright.

All trademarks mentioned within the pages of this book are the property of their respective owners.

In all other regards, copyright in the text of this book is held by me, David M. Milloy. Copyright in the cover illustrations is held by Russell J. Wallis.

ABOUT THE BOOK

This book contains questions: one hundred and thirty of them split into thirteen sections of ten.

So it's a quiz book, then?

Well, yes, except it's also a history book of sorts: for every multiple-choice question there's a corresponding story which offers facts, statistics and/or trivia relating to the question, the answer to it, or both.

So it's a bit more than just a quiz book.

As with the previous Ultimate books, this one sticks largely to facts. Unfortunately, in this day and age it's easy to copy and paste a 'fact' without actually verifying that it's accurate. That's not my way. As ever, I've done my best to ensure that the facts stated within this book are just that. All errors are, of course, down to me and me alone.

I do offer some (mostly flippant) opinions from time to time. Again, those are my sole responsibility.

This isn't the easiest quiz you'll ever have a crack at, but hopefully it'll be one of the most enjoyable and informative.

I hope you enjoy the book.

Have fun,

David M. Milloy
November, 2021

PART ONE
The questions

GENERAL KNOWLEDGE 1

1 What car was presented to Leonid Brezhnev by President Nixon at Camp David in 1973?

    A.   Cadillac Seville
    B.   Lincoln Continental
    C.   Chevrolet Monte Carlo
    D.   Chrysler Cordoba

2 By what name was the range of engines used by the Talbot Samba known?

    A.   Poissy
    B.   J
    C.   Cleon
    D.   X

3 What happened to the body dies used to produce panels for the DeLorean DMC-12?

    A.   They were used as anchors at a salmon farm
    B.   They were stolen after the DeLorean factory closed
    C.   They became museum exhibits in Belfast
    D.   They were melted down on the instructions of the UK government

4 Certain models of which car are known as 'Oscar India' versions?

    A.   Jaguar XJ-S
    B.   Aston Martin V8
    C.   Rolls-Royce Silver Shadow
    D.   Jensen Interceptor

5 In 1997, which car flipped over whilst undergoing the so-called 'elk test' in Sweden?

A. Renault Espace
B. Suzuki Jimny
C. Mercedes-Benz A Class
D. Jeep Cherokee

6 The slogan "Power is nothing without control" was used to advertise what?

A. Audi Quattro Coupe
B. Bilstein Shock Absorbers
C. Ferodo brake pads
D. Pirelli tyres

7 A modified version of which car set a world record speed of 172.4 mph for the Flying Mile at Jabbeke in Belgium in 1953?

A. Chevrolet Corvette
B. Jaguar XK120
C. Ferrari 375 America
D. Aston Martin DB2/4

8 Which item of bodywork did the Maxi share with the BMC 1800?

   A. Front wings
   B. Bonnet
   C. Doors
   D. Roof

9 At launch in 1975, the car that is best known as the Princess was available as an Austin, a Morris and a...?

   A. Rover
   B. Triumph
   C. Riley
   D. Wolseley

10 Rally driver Erik Carlsson was famously associated with which marque?

   A. Volvo
   B. Ford
   C. BMW
   D. Saab

FILM AND TELEVISION 2

1 Which of the following cars does James Bond drive in the film '*Dr. No*'?

    A.   Aston Martin DB2
    B.   Sunbeam Alpine
    C.   MGA Twin Cam
    D.   Austin-Healey 3000

2 What car does Johnny Aculard drive in the hammer horror film 'Dracula A.D. 1972'?

    A.   MGB
    B.   Lotus Elan
    C.   Reliant Scimitar
    D.   Triumph Stag

3 Which 1980s British TV drama series focused on the fictional *Associated British Motors*?

    A.   The Brothers
    B.   On The Line
    C.   Big Deal
    D.   Hot Metal

4 In the film '*The Day of The Jackal*', in which car does the Jackal cross the border from Italy to France?

    A.   Alfa Romeo Giulietta Spider
    B.   Peugeot 404 Cabriolet
    C.   Fiat 1200 Spyder
    D.   Lancia Appia Cabriolet

5 What car does Basil Fawlty attack with a tree branch in an episode of '*Fawlty Towers*'?

    A.   Austin Maxi
    B.   Austin Allegro Estate
    C.   Austin 1100 Countryman
    D.   Princess

6 In which of the following films does a Lotus Esprit NOT feature?

    A.   Moonraker
    B.   Basic Instinct
    C.   Pretty Woman
    D.   If Looks Could Kill

7 In what car do The Driver and The Mechanic make their way through the American Southwest in the in 1971 film '*Two Lane Blacktop*'?

    A.   Pontiac GTO
    B.   Buick Riviera
    C.   Chevrolet 150
    D.   Plymouth Superbird

8 In the final episode of the TV series '*Ashes to Ashes*', Gene Hunt is seen to flick through a brochure for which car?

- A. Audi Quattro
- B. BMW 323i
- C. Rover Vitesse
- D. Mercedes 190D

9 In the 1991 film '*Thelma & Louise*', in which car do the heroines attempt to escape to Mexico?

- A. Lincoln Continental Mark V convertible?
- B. Plymouth Satellite convertible
- C. Ford Thunderbird convertible
- D. Pontiac GTO convertible

10 In the 2001 film '*Swordfish*', what British car features in the car chase sequence?

- A. Lotus Turbo Esprit
- B. TVR Tuscan
- C. Aston Martin Vantage V600
- D. Jaguar XKR

IT'S A NUMBERS GAME

3

1 The number '340' in the Lotus 340R's name signifies?

- A. Its power to weight ratio in bhp per tonne.
- B. The number of days it took to develop from first sketch to production car
- C. The number of examples built
- D. It does not represent anything in particular.

2 What is the angle in degrees between the two banks of cylinders in Volkswagen's VR6 engine?

- A. 15
- B. 45
- C. 33
- D. 25

3 Once a common sight adjacent to UK roads, when did the last Little Chef restaurant close?

- A. 2018
- B. 2012
- C. 2016
- D. 2014

4 Which Audi was sold in the USA as the Fox?

- A. 90
- B. 50
- C. 80
- D. 100

5 In what year were the first EuroNCAP safety ratings published?

- A. 1997
- B. 2000
- C. 1995
- D. 2003

6 How much did cost to buy a Vauxhall Lotus Carlton on its UK launch in 1990?

- A. £39,000
- B. £54,000
- C. £48,000
- D. £35,000

7 As at 2021, which car has scored the highest number of votes in becoming European Car of the Year?

- A. Alfa Romeo 156
- B. Peugeot 405
- C. Lancia Delta
- D. Citroën XM

8 How many Chrysler Turbine Cars were built?

A. 40
B. 85
C. 70
D. 55

9 The strapline in a 1970s advert for which car stated "Takes you from 0 to the Magistrates Court in 11.4 seconds"?

A. Ford Capri 3.0S
B. Triumph Dolomite Sprint
C. MGB GT V8
D. TVR 3000M

10 To the nearest thousand, how many Lancia Gammas (Berlina and Coupe) were built?

A. 43000
B. 16000
C. 31000
D. 22000

GENERAL KNOWLEDGE 2

4

1 The Hillman Hunter GLS featured an engine tuned by...?

A. Downton
B. Piper
C. Holbay
D. Cosworth

2 The platform of the Aston Martin DB7 was based on that of which car?

A. Aston Martin Virage
B. Jaguar XK8
C. Ford Mustang
D. Jaguar XJS

3 The first Tesla road car was based on which other car?

A. Renault Spider
B. Lotus Elise
C. Toyota MR2 Spider
D. Hommell Barquette

4 What was the name of the British Rail service that transported passengers with their cars?

A. Railcar
B. Easydrive
C. Car Shuttle
D. Motorail

5 Bruce Forsyth appeared in a UK TV advertisement for which car?

- A. Chrysler Avenger
- B. Rover 213
- C. Nissan Sunny
- D. Austin Montego

6 Stylist Chris Bangle is best known for his work with which company?

- A. Fiat
- B. BMW
- C. Peugeot
- D. Porsche

7 At which motor show did the Mazda MX-5 make its debut?

- A. Geneva
- B. Chicago
- C. Tokyo
- D. Frankfurt

8 The Bellini sports car in the 1960 film 'School for Scoundrels' was really a disguised...?

    A.   Jaguar D-Type
    B.   Ferrari 250
    C.   Aston Martin DB3S
    D.   Maserati 3500 GT

9 As of 2021, the title of European Car of the Year has never been awarded to a car built by...?

    A.   BMW
    B.   Alfa Romeo
    C.   Mercedes-Benz
    D.   Volvo

10 Nigel Mansell and Tiff Needell both raced in British F3 in cars powered by which engine?

    A.   Triumph 2.0 litre 16 valve slant-four
    B.   Ford Pinto 2.0 litre
    C.   BL 'O' series 2.0 litre
    D.   Vauxhall slant-4 2.0 litre

MOTORSPORT 5

1 Which car took victory in the 1970 London to Mexico Rally?

- A. Hillman Hunter
- B. Mercedes-Benz 280SE
- C. Ford Escort
- D. Triumph 2500 Pi

2 Which of the following cars NEVER won the overall British Saloon Car Championship?

- A. Ford Capri 3000S
- B. Mini 1275 GTC.
- C. Alfa Romeo GTV6
- D. Rover Vitesse

3 Which tuning expert managed Dealer Team Vauxhall's racing and rallying programme?

- A. Dave Brodie
- B. Bill Blydenstein
- C. Stuart Turner
- D. Des O'Dell

4 What car did F1 and IndyCar champion Nigel Mansell drive in the 1993 TOCA Shootout?

- A. Renault 19
- B. Vauxhall Cavalier
- C. BMW 318
- D. Ford Mondeo

5 1976 F1 World Champion James Hunt later owned a van based on which car?

    A.   Austin A35
    B.   Hillman Husky
    C.   Morris Minor
    D.   Ford Anglia

6 Which F1 driver later worked for Lotus Engineering and played an important role in the development of several road cars for both Lotus and its clients?

    A.   Jim Crawford
    B.   Peter Gethin
    C.   John Miles
    D.   Brian Henton

7 How many BTCC race wins were scored by the Volvo 850 Estate?

    A.   Three
    B.   None
    C.   One
    D.   Two

8 In which car did Formula 1 team managers compete for the Jack Brabham Trophy in 1971?

    A.   Mini Cooper S
    B.   Ford Escort Mexico
    C.   Hillman Avenger Tiger
    D.   Ford Cortina Lotus

9 What was the MG Metro 6R4's best result in a round of the World Rally Championship?

    A.   Third
    B.   Sixth
    C.   Second
    D.   Fifth

10 Henri Toivonen drove which car to second place in the 1978 Arctic Rally?

    A.   Austin Allegro
    B.   Renault 20
    C.   Volkswagen Golf
    D.   Chrysler Avenger

IT PAYS TO ADVERTISE

6

1 The products of which car company were promoted on UK television by The Two Ronnies?

A. Ford
B. British Leyland
C. Chrysler
D. Vauxhall

2 Nicole and Papa were characters in UK television adverts for which car?

A. Peugeot 205
B. Renault 5
C. Citroën AX
D. Renault Clio

3 A song by which musical artist was used in UK television advertising for the Peugeot 206?

A. Seal
B. Lenny Kravitz
C. Terence Trent D'Arby
D. Roachford

4 Which French sports car was advertised using a slogan which translates as "The teeth of the road"?

A. Alpine GTA
B. Talbot-Matra Murena
C. Venturi Atlantique
D. Ligier JS2

5 Which American actor appeared in the 'New Rules' advertisements for the Vauxhall Vectra in 2002?

   A.   Kevin Bacon
   B.   Dennis Quaid
   C.   John Lithgow
   D.   Ed Harris

6 Which song was used in early UK television commercials for the Renault 21?

   A.   I Feel Free
   B.   You Can Go Your Own Way
   C.   Driven by You
   D.   Lust for Life

7 Who appeared in a UK TV commercial for the Chrysler Alpine and later went on to present 'Top Gear'?

   A.   Chris Goffey
   B.   Angela Rippon
   C.   William Woollard
   D.   Noel Edmonds

8 What car was advertised with the slogan "In and out like Ronald Biggs..."

    A.   Ford Fiesta
    B.   Talbot Samba
    C.   Vauxhall Nova
    D.   Mini

9 An aria from which opera was used in the UK television advert for the Fiat Strada?

    A.   The Barber of Seville
    B.   Tosca
    C.   La Boheme
    D.   La Traviata

10 According to its makers' advertising, what car was "The shape of things to come"?

    A.   Renault Avantime
    B.   Audi 100
    C.   Triumph TR7
    D.   Ford Sierra

GENERAL KNOWLEDGE 3

1 To the nearest thousand, how many examples of the Talbot Tagora were built?

- A. 20,000
- B. 25,000
- C. 15,000
- D. 10,000

2 Maurice Gatsonides, inventor of the Gatso speed camera, won which notable motorsport event?

- A. Targa Florio
- B. Monte Carlo Rally
- C. Paris-Dakar Rally
- D. Le Mans 24 Hours

3 Badged as a Lancia in many markets, what badge did the Y10 supermini sport in its home market?

- A. Fiat
- B. SEAT
- C. Autobianchi
- D. Innocenti

4 The Volkswagen Type 181 is known in the USA as the Volkswagen..?

- A. Caribe
- B. Rabbit
- C. Thing
- D. Kombi

5 The Hofstetter Turbo sports car was built in which country?

    A.   Brazil
    B.   Switzerland
    C.   Argentina
    D.   Austria

6 Which of the following Renault models lacked a Gordini version in its model range?

    A.   12
    B.   16
    C.   17
    D.   5

7 What was the first name of Lord Stokes, chairman of British Leyland from 1968 to 1975?

    A.   Herbert
    B.   Donald
    C.   Terence
    D.   Colin

8 Where was Bond Cars' factory situated?

- A. Preston
- B. Liverpool
- C. Tamworth
- D. Blackpool

9 Which of the following pop stars once worked at a car factory?

- A. David Bowie
- B. Billy Joel
- C. Paul Weller
- D. Bob Marley

10 Which F1 team did British Leyland sponsor?

- A. McLaren
- B. Brabham
- C. Tyrrell
- D. Williams

THE PEOPLE

8

1 All four members of the Beatles owned a Mini Cooper customised by which company?

- A. Downton
- B. Wood & Pickett
- C. Radford
- D. Ogle

2 Who crashed his McLaren F1 road car, reportedly resulting in an insurance payout of over £900,000?

- A. Richard Hammond
- B. Nick Mason
- C. James Martin
- D. Rowan Atkinson

3 Which former Jaguar chairman held Ministerial office as H.M. Paymaster General?

- A. Geoffrey Robinson
- B. Norman Tebbit
- C. Michael Jopling
- D. Stephen Byers

4 Tony Crook was the somewhat distinctive owner of which British car manufacturer?

- A. Bristol
- B. Gilbern
- C. Caterham
- D. Panther

5 John Glenn was ribbed by his fellow Mercury astronauts for owning which car?

    A.   Mini 850
    B.   Volkswagen Beetle
    C.   NSU Prinz
    D.   Simca 1000

6 Great Train Robber Bruce Reynolds bought which car (in cash) on the day after the robbery?

    A.   Jaguar Mark 2
    B.   Austin-Healey 3000
    C.   Jensen CV-8
    D.   Jaguar E-Type

7 The orange globes at UK pedestrian crossings were informally named after whom?

    A.   David Lloyd George
    B.   Leslie Hore-Belisha
    C.   Clement Atlee
    D.   Ernest Bevin

8 Major Ivan Hirst is credited with saving which car manufacturer?

- A. BMW
- B. Triumph
- C. Volkswagen
- D. Rolls-Royce

9 Which car formerly owned by Princess Diana sold at auction for £52,640 in 2021?

- A. Austin Metro HLS
- B. Ford Escort Ghia
- C. Audi A4 Cabriolet
- D. Ford Escort RS Turbo

10 Director John Boorman once took to the Pacific Coast Highway with whom on the roof of the car he was driving?

- A. Peter O'Toole
- B. Oliver Reed
- C. Lee Marvin
- D. Richard Harris

9

PROTOTYPES AND CONCEPTS

1 The Equus was a 1978 prototype built by which company?

A. British Leyland
B. Aston Martin
C. Jaguar
D. Vauxhall

2 In what year did a company then co-owned by British Leyland produce a prototype electric car based on a Mini platform?

A. 1970
B. 1974
C. 1972
D. 1968

3 The Talbot Wind was a one-off prototype created by which coachbuilder?

A. Figone et Falachi
B. Berliet
C. Heuliez
D. Chapron

4 What was the model designation of Porsche's 1980s small roadster project?

A. 972
B. 984
C. 976
D. 988

5 The original Panther Solo was to have been powered by which engine?

- A. Vauxhall 1.8 litre
- B. Ford 1.6 litre CVH
- C. 2.0 litre Rover 'O' series
- D. Fiat 2.0 litre twin-cam

6 Which design house was responsible for the 1972 Citroën GS Camargue 1972 prototype?

- A. Pininfarina
- B. Vignale
- C. Bertone
- D. Ogle

7 The Triplex 10-20 was a one-off shooting brake conversion of which car?

- A. Aston Martin V8
- B. Triumph TR7
- C. Jaguar XJS
- D. Princess

8 Which Ford concept car evolved into the Sierra?

A. Probe III
B. Coins
C. Megastar II
D. 021c

9 The Fiat X1/23 was a prototype...?

A. Sports car
B. MPV
C. Electric city car
D. Amphibious car

10 The Aston Martin DBS V8-based Sotheby Special was designed by...?

A. Trevor Fiore
B. William Towns
C. Robert Opron
D. Tom Karen

GENERAL KNOWLEDGE 4

10

1 Which prototype car was crashed by its test driver during filming in 1971?

- A. Rover BS
- B. Jaguar XJ13
- C. Aston Martin Bulldog
- D. Jensen F-Type

2 Which somewhat dilapidated car does Withnail drive in the 1987 film '*Withnail & I*'?

- A. Morris Oxford
- B. Jaguar Mark 2
- C. Rover 2000
- D. Austin Westminster

3 Which of the following cars did NOT feature at least one version powered by the Rover K-Series engine?

- A. Lotus Elise
- B. Land Rover Freelander
- C. Rover 600
- D. Reliant Scimitar Sabre

4 The Alfa Romeo Montreal prototypes shown at the 1967 World's Fair were fitted with which engine?

- A. 1570cc 4-cylinder
- B. 1995cc V8
- C. 1779cc 4-cylinder
- D. 2593cc V8

5 Which of these Volkswagen saloons was the first to go on sale?

A. Santana
B. Bora
C. Derby
D. Jetta

6 Louis Malle's 1973 documentary film '*Humain*', trop '*humain*' focused on which car manufacturer?

A. Renault
B. Simca
C. Peugeot
D. Citroën

7 In 1965, which car set a record by achieving sales of over 1,000,000 examples in the USA in a single year?

A. Ford Thunderbird
B. Chevrolet Impala
C. Dodge Polara
D. Mercury Monterey

8 In which country was height-adjustable suspension banned from 1974 to 1981?

A. Japan
B. Norway
C. New Zealand
D. USA

9 Which Porsche was reintroduced to the range six years after its deletion?

A. 914
B. 912
C. 924
D. 356

10 In what year did TVR's factory at Blackpool close?

A. 2010
B. 2006
C. 2013
D. 2008

LESSER SPOTTED CLASSICS

11

1 The Panther Rio was based on which car?

- A. Triumph Dolomite
- B. Ford Granada
- C. Rover 3500
- D. Vauxhall VX 4/90

2 The Fiesta Fly convertible was originally produced by which company?

- A. Torcars
- B. Crayford
- C. Hodec
- D. Danbury

3 What Rover Group car was offered as a 'BRM' limited edition?

- A. MG TF
- B. MG ZS
- C. Rover 600
- D. Rover 200

4 Which animal featured on the Gordon-Keeble marque badge?

- A. Tortoise
- B. Kestrel
- C. Hare
- D. Deer

5 The Indian-made Sipani Dolphin was based on which European car?

A. Fiat Panda
B. Peugeot LNA
C. Reliant Kitten
D. SEAT 600

6 What was the name given to the styling of the Triumph Mayflower?

A. New Edge
B. Flame Surfaced
C. Razor Edge
D. New Elizabethan

7 The Campero was a Spanish-built utility vehicle based on which car?

A. Fiat 127
B. Simca 1200
C. Renault 12
D. Opel Kadett

8 What was the model designation of the first car produced by Noble Automotive?

- A. M10
- B. M1
- C. M12
- D. M100

9 Torcars of Devon offered a camper van conversion of which car?

- A. Maxi
- B. Princess
- C. Austin Allegro
- D. Morris Marina

10 How many examples of the Peugeot 405 T16 were produced?

- A. 217
- B. 1046
- C. 1865
- D. 693

UNITED STATES OF AMERICA

12

1 Which 1950s American car was built in the UK and sold in the USA as a captive import?

A. Packard 200
B. Nash Metropolitan
C. Studebaker Scotsman
D. Buick Roadmaster Skylark

2 Which US car was popularly known as '*the goat*'?

A. Dodge Charger
B. Pontiac GTO
C. Chevrolet Camaro Z28
D. AMC AMX

3 The Renault 11 was sold in the USA as the Renault...?

A. Alliance
B. Entente
C. Encore
D. Cordiale

4 Which US company was best known for manufacturing taxi cabs?

A. LaFayette
B. Stutz
C. Lexington
D. Checker

5 Which car was pictured with the Apollo 12 crew in '*Life*' magazine?

    A.   Dodge Challenger
    B.   Chevrolet Corvette
    C.   Plymouth Barracuda
    D.   Ford Mustang

6 The Mitsubishi Starion was marketed in the US by Chrysler, Dodge and Plymouth as the...?

    A.   Carousel
    B.   Challenger
    C.   Champion
    D.   Conquest

7 What was the name of the range of all-wheel drive cars introduced by AMC in 1979?

    A.   Eagle
    B.   Hornet
    C.   Vixen
    D.   Bobcat

8 In which US State will you find the art installation known as the Cadillac Ranch?

- A. Arizona
- B. Nevada
- C. Texas
- D. New Mexico

9 Which of the following US marques was the first to disappear from new car showrooms?

- A. Plymouth
- B. AMC
- C. Studebaker
- D. Packard

10 The EV1 was an electric car produced by which manufacturer?

- A. Ford
- B. General Motors
- C. Chrysler
- D. Tesla

13

FIRST AND LAST

1 What was the first production car to feature remote-controlled central locking?

A. Renault 9
B. Renault 30
C. Renault 21
D. Renault Fuego

2 What was the last Alfa Romeo to enter production before the company became part of Fiat?

A. 75
B. Arna
C. 33
D. 1643

3 In what year did the first mass-produced Ford to have front-wheel drive go into production?

A. 1967
B. 1962
C. 1979
D. 1976

4 In what year did Nissan cease to use the Datsun brand name in the UK?

A. 1984
B. 1986
C. 1990
D. 1988

5 In which production car did rally ace Tony Pond lap the Isle of Man TT circuit at an average speed of over 100 mph?

- A. Ford Sierra Cosworth
- B. Audi 90 Quattro
- C. Rover 827 Vitesse
- D. Subaru Legacy

6 In what year was '*Motor*' magazine absorbed into Autocar?

- A. 1990
- B. 1994
- C. 1982
- D. 1988

7 Whose company was the first to offer a V8-engined version of the MGB?

- A. Ken Costello
- B. Brian Hart
- C. Keith Duckworth
- D. Ron Gammons

8 What was the last Citroën car to be introduced with an air-cooled engine?

A. Axel
B. Visa
C. GSA
D. AX

9 The prancing horse seen on Ferrari's logo was originally used by ...?

A. Luigi Becalli, winner of the 1932 Olympic 1500m
B. Inigo Camponi, Italian naval officer executed in 1944
C. Count Francesco Baracca, WW1 fighter ace
D. Ugo Sivocci, winner of the 1923 Targa Florio

10 What make of car was on board RMS Titanic when she made her ill-fated maiden voyage?

A. Peugeot
B. Daimler
C. Renault
D. Rolls-Royce

PART TWO
The answers

1 GENERAL KNOWLEDGE 1 : Answers

1. B. Lincoln Continental
2. D. X
3. A. They were used as anchors at a salmon farm
4. B. Aston Martin V8
5. C. Mercedes-Benz A Class
6. D. Pirelli tyres
7. B. Jaguar XK120
8. C. Doors
9. D. Wolseley
10. D. Saab

2 FILM AND TELEVISION : Answers

1. B. Sunbeam Alpine
2. D. Triumph Stag
3. B. On The Line
4. A. Alfa Romeo Giulietta Spider
5. C. Austin 1100 Countryman
6. A. Moonraker
7. C. Chevrolet 150
8. D. Mercedes 190D
9. C. Ford Thunderbird convertible
10. B. TVR Tuscan

3 IT'S A NUMBERS GAME : Answers

1. C.   The number of examples built
2. A.   15
3. A.   2018
4. C.   80
5. A.   1997
6. C.   £48000
7. B.   Peugeot 405
8. D.   55
9. B.   Triumph Dolomite Sprint
10. D. 22000

4 GENERAL KNOWLEDGE 2 : Answers

1. C.   Holbay
2. D.   Jaguar XJS
3. B.   Lotus Elise
4. D.   Motorail
5. A.   Chrysler Avenger
6. B.   BMW
7. B.   Chicago
8. C.   Aston Martin DB3S
9. A.   BMW
10. A. Triumph 2.0 litre 16 valve slant-four

5 MOTORSPORT : Answers

1. C. Ford Escort
2. A. Ford Capri 3000S
3. B. Bill Blydenstein
4. D. Ford Mondeo
5. A. Austin A35
6. C. John Miles
7. B. None
8. B. Ford Escort Mexico
9. A. Third
10. D. Chrysler Avenger

6 IT PAYS TO ADVERTISE : Answers

1. B. British Leyland
2. D. Renault Clio
3. B. Leny Kravitz
4. B. Talbot-Matra Murena
5. D. Ed Harris
6. A. I Feel Free
7. C. William Woollard
8. D. Mini
9. A. The Barber of Seville
10. C. Triumph TR7

7 GENERAL KNOWLEDGE 3 : Answers

1. A. 20,000
2. B. Monte carlo Rally
3. C. Autobianchi
4. C. Thing
5. A. Brazil
6. B. 16
7. B. Donald
8. A. Preston
9. D. Bob Marley
10. D. Willams

8 THE PEOPLE : Answers

1. C. Radford
2. D. Rowan Atkinson
3. A. Geoffrey Robinson
4. A. Bristol
5. C. NSU Prinz
6. B. Austin-Healey 3000
7. B. Leslie Hore-Belisha
8. C. Volkswagen
9. B. Ford Escort Ghia
10. C. Lee Marvin

9 PROTOTYPES AND CONCEPTS : Answers

1. D. Vauxhall
2. C. 1972
3. C. Heuliez
4. B. 984
5. B. Ford 1.6 litre CVH
6. C. Bertone
7. D. Princess
8. A. Probe III
9. C. Electric city car
10. D. Tom Karen

10 GENERAL KNOWLEDGE 4 : Answers

1. B. Jaguar XJ13
2. D. Jaguar Mark 2
3. C. Rover 600
4. A. 1570cc 4-cylinder
5. C. Derby
6. D. Citroën
7. B. Chevrolet Impala
8. D. USA
9. B. 912
10. B. 2006

11 LESSER SPOTTED CLASSICS : Answers

1. A. Triumph Dolomite
2. B. Crayford
3. D. Rover 200
4. A. Tortoise
5. C. Reliant Kitten
6. C. Razor Edge
7. B. Simca 1200
8. A. M10
9. D. Morris Marina
10. B. 1046

12 UNITED STATES OF AMERICA : Answers

1. B. Nash Metropolitan
2. B. Pontiac GTO
3. C. Encore
4. D. Checker
5. B. Chevrolet Corvette
6. D. Conquest
7. A. Eagle
8. C. Texas
9. D. Packard
10. B. General Motors

13 FIRST AND LAST : Answers

1. D. Renault Fuego
2. A. 75
3. B. 1962
4. A. 1984
5. C. Rover 827 Vitesse
6. D. 1988
7. A. Ken Costello
8. A. Axel
9. C. Count Francesco Baracca, WW1 fighter ace.
10. C. Renault

PART THREE
The stories behind the answers

1

GENERAL KNOWLEDGE 1

Q1. *What car was presented to Leonid Brezhnev by President Nixon at Camp David in 1973?*

B. Lincoln Continental

As noted in The Ultimate Classic Car Quiz Book, Leonid Brezhnev loved cars. So much so, in fact, that he amassed a collection of them that would put many a museum to shame.

He was often presented with cars on his foreign trips. This was true of his visit to the USA in 1973 for a Summit with US President Richard Nixon. Having initially convened at The White House, the two leaders and their entourages travelled to Camp David in Maryland. There, Nixon presented Brezhnev with a brand new Lincoln Continental with dark blue paintwork and black velour upholstery.

Keen to try out his new car, Brezhnev (with Nixon in the passenger seat) took it for an impromptu test session around the perimeter roads of Camp David. As the car sped towards a sharp downhill turn, the somewhat concerned US President beseeched his Soviet counterpart to slow down. To the relief of all, however, Brezhnev was a sufficiently accomplished driver to make the turn without damage to either the car or its very high value cargo.

The Lincoln survives to this day and is on display at the Riga Motor Museum in Latvia.

Q2. *By what name was the range of engines used by the Talbot Samba known?*

D. X

Launched in 1981, the Talbot Samba holds the distinction of being the last new Talbot-badged car to be launched.

Introduced as a replacement for the Talbot Sunbeam, the Samba was essentially a revised version of the Peugeot 104 rather than an all-new car. As such, it was powered by the Peugeot/Renault X engine rather than either the venerable Rootes engines which had powered the Sunbeam or the equally venerable Simca engines found in the Samba's larger stablemates, the Talbot Horizon and Talbot 1510 (a.k.a. Talbot Alpine).

In addition to the Samba, versions of the X engine saw service in a number of Peugeots and Citroëns as well as the Renault 14. The X engine is often referred to as the Douvrin engine (it is not, however, the only engine to be so named) because of the town in which it was built. More colourfully, however, it became known to many as the suitcase engine.

Q3. *What happened to the dies used to produce panels for the DeLorean DMC-12?*

A. **They were used as anchors at a salmon farm**

The DMC-12's stainless steel body panels were not fabricated at Dunmurry but by a German company, August Lapple Gbmh. One panel was made in Germany and shipped to Ireland but the remainder were fabricated at their plant in Carlow in the Republic of Ireland.

When DeLorean Motor Company Limited went into liquidation, Lapple was not only owed money that it was unlikely to recover but was the possessor of heavy (some weighed around 25 tonnes) and expensive tools which were now surplus to requirements.

Some of the smaller tools were melted down but others were sold to scrap dealers throughout Ireland. Of these, twelve were transported by ship to Kilkerian Bay, Galway, where they were used as anchors at a fish farm.

The fish farm itself is no longer in operation but the dies remain at the bottom of the bay, corroded and covered with marine life.

Q4. *Certain models of which car are known as 'Oscar India' versions?*

B.   Aston Martin V8

If you've ever wondered why some older Aston Martin cars are referred to as 'Oscar India' models then wonder no longer.

The answer is that it refers to the version of the car first launched in October of 1978, or in other words to an 'October Introduction'. But what's the link between those two words and *Oscar India?* Well, take the first letter of October and the first letter of *Introduction* and convert them to the phonetic alphabet. Thus *O* becomes *Oscar* and *I* becomes *India*.

It's simple albeit rather pointless. Still, at least the car was good.

Q5. *In 1997, which car flipped over whilst undergoing the so-called 'elk test' in Sweden?*

C.   Mercedes-Benz A Class

The 'elk test' is a fairly simple test of a vehicle's ability to avoid an obstacle that suddenly appears in front of it. Regularly used in Sweden and several other northern countries, the test has been around for many years.

It gained its current name following a well-publicised incident in 1997, when the then-new Mercedes-Benz A-Class flipped onto its roof whilst attempting the manoeuvre in the hands of Swedish journalist Robin Collin. When Collin subsequently spoke about the accident to a German newspaper, *Süddeutsche Zeitung*, he referred to the test as being one that simulated the sort of manoeuvre that might be necessary to avoid a moose in the road.

For Mercedes-Benz, the episode was both embarrassing and expensive, with the fix adopted by the company reputedly costing 300 million Euros.

Q6. *The slogan "Power is nothing without control" was used to advertise what?*

D. Pirelli tyres

This classic slogan first appeared in 1994 as the text to a photograph by Annie Leibovitz which depicted former World and Olympic 100 metre champion Carl Lewis about to start a race with a pair of red stilettos on his feet rather than running shoes.

It was later followed by a video that showed Lewis, now with rubber treads on the soles of his feet, running on water and sprinting up the side of the Statue of Liberty.

Q7. *A modified version of which car set a world record speed of 172.4 mph for the Flying Mile at Jabbeke in Belgium in 1953?*

B. Jaguar XK120

Launched in 1948, the Jaguar XK 120 was not only the marque's first post-war sports car but also the first production car to feature the brand new XK engine.

Although the '120' in its name referred to the XK 120's claimed top speed, Jaguar decided to show that it was, with certain modifications, capable of more. Accordingly, the company arranged for some timed speed runs to be conducted on a stretch of motorway at Jabbeke in Belgium.

The first runs, conducted in 1949, resulted in an XK120 (with a small windshield replacing its windscreen) attaining an average speed of 132.6 mph over a flying mile. The addition of a tonneau cover over the passenger's side of the cockpit saw that figure rise to 135.0 miles per hour.

In 1953, Jaguar returned to Jabbeke with a more substantially modified XK120. This car a featured an engine with a higher than standard compression ratio, a close-ratio gearbox, streamlined headlamps, a full underbody cover, over-inflated tyres that had only 2mm of tread, and aerodynamic alterations that included a bubble-shaped canopy and a metal tonneau cover. Driven by test driver Norman Dewis, this XK120 achieved an average speed of 172.4 mph over the flying mile, thus setting a new world record.

Dewis's record breaking XK120 was thereafter converted back to road car specification and sold, at one point being owned by racing driver Brian Redman. It was subsequently restored to its record-breaking specification and remains in this guise today.

Q8. *Which item of bodywork did the Maxi share with the Austin 1800?*

C.   **Doors**

At launch in 1969, the Maxi broke new ground for a British car by featuring a four door plus opening hatchback configuration.

Compared to its larger sibling, colloquially known as the Landcrab, the Maxi was smaller, lighter, and much more space efficient. It was, however, somewhat lacking in the looks department. Although this was largely attributable to its makers' conservative approach to styling, its case wasn't helped by being burdened – due to budgetary constraints – with doors from the larger Landcrab. The result was a car that not only resembled its bigger stablemate (not a good thing) but also one that had a fairly large wheelbase relative to its overall length.

Like most BL offerings of the time, the Maxi had to soldier on for rather longer than ought to have been the case. It might have been a different story if funds had been available to properly update the Maxi, but as it turned out one of the the biggest changes came in 1977 when the Austin prefix was dropped pursuant to a recommendation in the Ryder Report. Thereafter, it was largely left to fend for itself against newer and better competition.

Lord Stokes had said in 1969 that the Maxi would be around "at least for another 10 years". In the event, it remained in production until 1981, by which time its appeal – and sales - had waned.
Oh, and lest you wonder, it was still lumbered with the same doors when the end came…

Q9. *At launch in 1975, the car that is best known as the Princess was available as an Austin, a Morris and a…?*

D.   Wolseley

You might find this hard to believe. No, scratch that. Unless you're new to the world of British Leyland, you won't find it hard to believe that British Leyland decided to fly in the face of logic, reason and the winds of change by deciding that their wedge-shaped new family car would have a traditional boot rather than a hatchback.

This act of folly came close to being equalled by BL's decision to offer the new car (which we'll call the 'wedge') with one of three different marque badges: Austin, Morris and Wolseley. There were some differences between the three, but these were minor to the point of insignificance.

Following the publication of the Ryder Report in March 1975, a degree of much-needed rationalisation was introduced at British Leyland. One effect of this was the relaunch of the wedge in September 1975 with a new name: Princess.

A revised version of the Princess, the Princess 2, appeared in 1978. The new O-Series engine replaced the B-Series on the four-cylinder models but there was still no hatchback. Three years later, the Princess finally gained a hatchback...and another new name. In this, its final incarnation, it was known as the Austin Ambassador. Production ended in 1984.

Q10. ***Rally driver Erik Carlsson was famously associated with which marque?***

D.   Saab

I should really have offered a bonus point for those able to name his brother-in-law! But since I didn't, I'll just say that Carlsson was married to Pat Moss - sister of Stirling Moss, and a talented rally driver in her own right.

As for Erik Carlsson, or Erik 'on the roof' Carlsson as he was often called, his name became synonymous with Saab, for whom he won the Monte Carlo Rally three times and the RAC Rally twice. The 1962 running of the latter event gave rise to a remarkable tale: a suspension component broke on Carlsson's Saab 96, making it appear inevitable that he would have to retire from the rally. However, by a remarkable stroke of good fortune he spotted a parked 96 road car. No-one was in the parked Saab, so Carlsson and his co-driver David Stone jacked it up, removed the necessary part, fitted it to his rally car, left a note on the parked Saab's windscreen, and continued on their way to victory. And just to complete a happy picture, the owner of the parked Saab ended up on friendly terms with Carlsson.

As for the 'on the roof' nickname, a series of Swedish children's books featured a character called Karlsson-on-the-roof. So it was perhaps natural that when one of Erik Carlsson's rally Saabs ended up on its roof (notwithstanding his phenomenal car control) he should be given the 'on the roof' soubriquet.

Q1. *Which of the following cars does James Bond drive in the film 'Dr. No'?*

B. Sunbeam Alpine

Although it was the first of the James Bond novels to be filmed, *Dr. No* was in fact the sixth of Ian Fleming's novels about the British secret agent.

Had Hollywood filmed the Fleming novels in the sequence in which they were published, it's probable that Bond would have been seen at the wheel of a Bentley. After all, he drove a 4.5 litre Blower Bentley in his first three outings in print: *Casino Royale, Live and Let Die,* and *Moonraker.*

The Blower was written off in the *Moonraker* novel but was replaced by a Mark VI. Like the earlier car, it was Battleship Grey. Bond thereafter seems to have acquired a Mark II Continental Bentley, which is mentioned from time to time in some of Fleming's later Bond stories.

There is, however, no mention of a Bentley in the *Dr. No* novel. Instead, Bond drove an early Sunbeam Alpine, a Hillman Minx, and that avatar of performance motoring: an Austin A30! Although Bond drove a Sunbeam Alpine in the film, it was a much later and more modern vehicle than in the book. Still, at least an Alpine made the transition from page to screen, unlike the Minx and A30.

Bond did briefly share a scene with a Bentley in the second film in the series, *From Russia With Love.* However, it was the wrong car (a 4¼ litre drophead) in the wrong colour (green) and appears to have been issued to Bond rather than being his property.

And that was pretty much that for Bond's on-screen relationship with Bentleys. A pity, but who knows what the future may hold...

Q2. *What car does Johnny Aculard drive in the Hammer Horror film 'Dracula A.D. 1972'?*

D. Triumph Stag

Apart from old big teeth himself, Johnny Aculard (the clue's in the name) is the main villain in Hammer's first attempt to bring the Dracula story into the modern (well, it was then) era.

A thoroughly bad egg, Aculard nonetheless makes a good fist of pretending to be a hip young man about London town, what with his very desirable mews home and his yellow Triumph Stag. One assumes that since the Stag isn't actually seen with steam pouring from its engine bay that some kind of magic spell has been placed upon it...

The Stag used in the film was a pre-production example. BL had obviously worked hard at product placement, as another yellow pre-production Stag was used in the James Bond film *Diamonds are Forever*.

Q3. *Which 1980s British TV drama series focused on the fictitious Associated British Motors?*

B. On The Line

There's not much I can say about this one. It's largely been forgotten, to the extent that it seems not to have been released on either VHS or DVD.

What I can tell you is that it was a primetime ITV drama series that ran for 13 episodes in 1982, and that its plot lines centred around a British car manufacturer, *Associated British Motors*.

There was a car too, the ABM *Orbit*. But whereas many of the series's plot lines were clearly influenced by the struggles of British Leyland, the car on which the Orbit was based was the mark 1 Ford Fiesta.

You can find images of the *Orbit* online. All I'll say about them is that there's a reason why the Fiesta's nose and tail didn't look like those of the *Orbit*!

Q4. *In the film 'The Day of The Jackal', in which car does the Jackal cross the border from Italy to France?*

A. Alfa Romeo Giulietta Spider

Although filmed in 1972, *The Day of The Jackal* was largely set a decade or so earlier.

A tense, well-shot thriller, its period setting means that whilst cars play a largely incidental role in the film, the ones that do appear on screen are appealing to classic car fans.

This is particularly true of the car that The Jackal uses to travel from Italy into France, a white Alfa Romeo Giulietta Spider. The Jackal later treats to the Alfa to a very professional looking respray (from rattle cans...), changing its colour to blue in an attempt to throw pursuers off his trail.

Q5. *What car does Basil Fawlty attack with a tree branch in an episode of 'Fawlty Towers'?*

C. Austin 1100 Countryman

Fawlty Towers is a classic 1970s sit-com which both stars and was co-written by John Cleese. In it, Cleese plays Basil Fawlty, a snobbish and misanthropic hotelier whose attempts to climb the social ladder invariably end up in farce.

In the episode entitled *Gourmet Nights*, Fawlty hopes to raise the standing of his establishment (and him with it) by hosting special gourmet nights in the hotel restaurant, the advertisement for which stated 'No riff-raff'.

Fawlty's plans soon hit a snag, however, when the hotel's new chef gets drunk. In desperation, Fawlty surreptitiously orders food from a local restaurant to feed to his expectant diners. Having collected the food from the restaurant, Fawlty's car - a red Austin 1100 Countryman - cuts out on the way back to the hotel and refuses to restart. This leads to a memorable scene in which Fawlty first threatens the 1100 before giving it, in his words, "a damn good thrashing" with a tree branch.

Q6. *In which of the following films does a Lotus Esprit NOT feature?*

A. Moonraker

There was a time when the Lotus Esprit appeared in several big-budget films, including *Basic Instinct*, *Pretty Woman* and *If Looks Could Kill* as well as two James Bond films.

Having made its debut (in S1 guise) in 1977's *The Spy Who Loved Me*, the Esprit (in Turbo form) also served as one of Bond's conveyances in *For Your Eyes Only* in 1981. It was, however, absent from the 1979 Bond film, *Moonraker*.

Mind you, with much of Moonraker's plot taking place in space, Bond didn't have much use for an Esprit during the film. After all, although the Esprit is great as a car and seemingly makes for a good submarine, its credentials as a spacecraft have yet to be established!

Q7. *In what car do The Driver and The Mechanic make their way through the American Southwest in the 1971 film 'Two-Lane Blacktop'?*

C. Chevrolet 150

Best described as an existential road movie, *Two-Lane Blacktop* features musicians James Taylor and Dennis Wilson in starring roles.

Its plot centres around two characters known only as The Driver (Taylor) and The Mechanic (Wilson), who drive around in their customised Chevrolet 150, taking part in one-on-one street drag races, the loser of which hands his car – and its ownership document (called 'the pink slip' in America) – to the winner.

Q8. *In the final episode of the TV series 'Ashes to Ashes', Gene Hunt is seen to flick through a brochure for which car?*

D. Mercedes 190D

Although Gene Hunt drove a mark 3 Cortina GXL in both series of *Life on Mars*, the predecessor of *Ashes to Ashes*, it is the red Audi Quattro that he drove in the latter show that became most closely associated with him. Indeed, such was the link between car and character that the UK Labour party used a pastiche of it in a poster for their 2010 General Election campaign, to fairly disastrous effect!

After Hunt's Quattro was wrecked in the final episode of *Ashes to Ashes*, viewers might have expected him to get hold of another Quattro, or at least another highly regarded performance car of that era. The scriptwriters had other ideas, however, and Hunt was instead seen to flick through a brochure for the Mercedes 190D – a curious choice, given that the 190D was much slower and considerably less visually appealing than the Quattro. Somehow, I just can't see him bellowing, "Fire up the 190D..."

Q9. *In the 1991 film 'Thelma & Louise', in which car do the heroines attempt to escape to Mexico?*

C. Ford Thunderbird convertible

For petrolheads, the real star of *Thelma & Louise* is neither Susan Sarandon nor Geena Davis nor director Ridley Scott. It isn't even the often striking scenery that acts as a backdrop to the action. Instead, centre stage is taken by the 1966 Ford Thunderbird convertible that features throughout much of the film, including its pedal-to-the-metal ending.

In actuality, several identical Thunderbirds were used for shooting, two of which were used for stunt sequences. In 2021, Sarandon and Davis were reunited with one of the Thunderbirds from the film at a reunion to celebrate the film's 30th anniversary. That particular Thunderbird is the property of the Petersen Automotive Museum in Los Angeles and is on display in the museum's Vault section.

According to Sarandon, it wasn't the only Thunderbird to have survived filming, as director Ridley Scott gave the other intact Thunderbirds from the film to relatives. Lucky them.

Q10. *In the 2001 film 'Swordfish', what British car features in the car chase sequence?*

B. TVR Tuscan

For all their rugged visual and aural appeal, TVRs have seldom been featured in major films. But there is one notable exception: *Swordfish*, a 2001 action film starring John Travolta, Hugh Jackman, and Halle Berry.

In the film, Travolta's British-registered, right-hand drive TVR Tuscan Speed Six (which was never sold in the USA) features in a chase sequence through night-time Los Angeles, in which credibility is strained beyond breaking point by the failure of the Tuscan (capable of over 175 mph and of accelerating from rest to 100 mph in under 10 seconds) to outrun the large SUVs (Lincoln Navigators and Ford Expeditions) that pursue it...

It's understood that six Tuscans were used in the filming of Swordfish, at least three of which survived the experience.

Q1. *The number '340' in the Lotus 340R's name signifies?*

C. The number of examples built

Lotus caused quite a stir at the 1998 British Motor Show in Birmingham, by showing off an Elise-based concept car, the 340R.

The styling of the 340R was raw and visceral, and the car itself lacked such niceties as opening doors, luggage space, and side windows. It had no roof nor made provision for one. The bodywork, such as there was, was made of composite materials, and the mechanical components at the rear of the car were exposed.

Like standard Elises, the 340R was powered by a 1.8 litre Rover K|Series engine. In the 340R's ultra-lightweight concept car form, the 190 bhp of its engine was enough, said Lotus, to give it a power to weight ration of 340bhp per tonne. Hence its name.

Unsurprisingly, there was a great deal of interest in the 340R. So much so, in fact, that Lotus decided to put it into production. However, transforming it from a concept car into one that was road legal meant having to make changes to it that both added weight and sapped a little of its power, which was down to 177 bhp.

And that meant that a road legal 340R (even the ones that left the factory with their engines uprated to 187 bhp) could not hope to achieve the spectacular power to weight ratio of the concept car.

How, then, could it keep its name?

Lotus's answer was a simple one: build 340 examples. And that's exactly what they did.

Q2. *What is the angle in degrees between the two banks of cylinders in Volkswagen's VR6 engine?*

A. **15**

Introduced in 1991, the Volkswagen VR6 engine is noted for having a very shallow angle of 15 degrees between its two banks of cylinders. This allows the cylinders to be contained in a single cylinder head making the engine both more compact and lighter than most V6 engines, which normally have a considerably greater angle (60 degrees is common) between their cylinder banks, necessitating the use of separate cylinder heads for each bank of three cylinders.

Volkswagen wasn't, however, the first manufacturer to produce a road car with an engine whose cylinders were arranged in a shallow 'V' configuration. That honour belongs to Lancia's V4 engine which was introduced in 1922 and had a 20 degree angle between banks.

The Volkswagen VR6 engine's most noted application was in the Corrado coupé from 1992 to 1995. It was, however, far from the engine's only application, as it appeared in a succession of Volkswagen Audi Group cars over the years. However, the drive towards smaller and cleaner internal combustion engines has resulted in the phasing out of the VR6 engine in favour of smaller capacity turbocharged units. VR6 units can, however, still be found in several Volkswagens made primarily for the Chinese market.

Q3. *Once a common sight adjacent to UK roads, when did the last Little Chef restaurant close?*

A. **2018**

It's fair to say that in its heyday, the Little Chef was something of a British institution.

Inspired by American diners and particularly noted for its range of all-day breakfasts, the Little Chef grew from a single restaurant near Reading in 1958 to a chain that covered the UK. At its peak, there were over 450 Little Chef restaurants in the United Kingdom, with a further five in the Republic of Ireland. The brand even made limited forays into France and Spain.

Little Chefs were invariably found adjacent to A-class or arterial roads, drawing their customer base primarily from motorists. Operating as part of a chain, Little Chef restaurants featured a standardised menu, some elements of which – such as the Olympic Breakfast and Jubilee Pancake – achieved what marketing people would today call significant brand penetration.

By the turn of the millennium, however, Little Chef was facing a number of challenges, including an increased level of competition and a perception that its food was overpriced. Following several changes of ownership and the closure of over 200 restaurants, Little Chef went into administration in December 2006. A new owner was quickly found, but the chain's downward spiral continued, notwithstanding a revamp that involved celebrity chef Heston Blumenthal.

A further change of ownership and another revamp failed to save the brand, and in February 2017 Little Chef's owners sold the existing Little Chef premises but not the brand's intellectual property and franchise control rights. The result of this was the rebranding or closure of all of the Little Chef outlets by early 2018.

In spite of the fact that there are currently (October 2021) no operational Little Chefs, the Little Chef website (www.littlechef.co.uk) continues to function with accessible menus, price lists and even details of and directions to the restaurants which were operational at the very start of 2017 but have long-since closed.

Q4. Which Audi was sold in the USA as the Fox?

C. 80

Launched in 1973, the Audi 80 was known by another name in North America: the Audi Fox. This led to a somewhat odd situation, whereby the Volkswagen Group sold both a Fox and a Rabbit (a.k.a. the VW Golf) in North America!

Be that as it may, the Fox name lasted until 1980, when it was replaced by a new name: the Audi 4000. This tag lasted until 1987, after which it became known as the Audi 90. In Europe, however, the Audi 80 name continued to be used until the model's eventual demise in the mid-90s.

There was also an Audi 90 in Europe from 1987 onwards. In Europe, the 90 shared the 80s bodyshell but had a slightly more upmarket specification.

The Audi 80 name was never used in North America, as the successor to both the 80 and 90 ranges carried a new name: the Audi A4. And unlike its predecessor, the A4 name was used on both sides of the Atlantic Ocean.

Q5. In what year were the first EuroNCAP safety ratings published?

A. 1997

Euro NCAP is a voluntary organisation which conducts standardised safety tests on new motor vehicles and issues results using both detailed reports and an at-a-glance rating system. There is no compulsion on manufacturers to submit cars for testing, as all new cars sold in Europe are required to be certified via the mandatory Type Approval system.

Euro NCAP is modelled on the New Car Assessment Program introduced in the USA in 1979 by the National Highway Traffic Safety Administration. However, Euro NCAP wasn't formed until November 1996, when the Swedish National Road Administration and the Federation Internationale de l'Automobile teamed up with the UK Department of Transport.

The first Euro NCAP report and ratings were presented in February, 1997, following the undertaking of safety tests on seven superminis. A second set of test results were published in July of that year, when the Volvo S40 became the first car to attain a 4-star rating for occupant protection. Since then, Euro NCAP's story has been one of growth and evolution, with new and improved tests being introduced on a regular basis.

Oh, and in case you're wondering, Euro NCAP stands for 'European New Car Assessment Programme'.

Q6. *How much did it cost to buy a Vauxhall Lotus Carlton on its UK launch in 1990?*

C.   £48,000

It was the car the tabloids hated and car thieves loved, the ultimate Q car: a four-door saloon that could attain almost 180 miles per hour and outstrip anything that UK police forces had at their disposal.

That it existed at all was due to the simple expedient of General Motors owning both Lotus and Vauxhall. Lotus did the development working, turning the 3.0 litre engine from the Carlton GSi into a twin-turbocharged 3.6 litre unit that produced 377 bhp and a veritable wall of torque. The Norfolk company also modified the Carlton's suspension, gave it bigger and more powerful brakes, and added a limited-slip differential.

When it was launched in 1990, the tabloids were somewhat outraged by the notion that anyone (well, anyone with £48,000 in their pocket) could buy a saloon car with such visceral performance, the police were concerned about their inability to catch it, and even the editor of *Autocar* opined that its top speed should be electronically limited to 155 mph. Indeed, such was the furore that both the *Daily Mail* and the A*ssociation of Chief Police Officers* campaigned to have it banned.

The Carlton was not, however, banned, even though it did become popular with car thieves. Indeed, in 1993 a stolen Carlton was used in a number of ram raids, leading a Bromsgrove police officer to state, "We simply haven't been able to get near the thing and it looks unlikely that we ever will." He was right: the police never did catch either the car or the thieves.

Q7. *As at 2021, which car has scored the highest number of votes in becoming European Car of the Year?*

B. Peugeot 405

1988 was a good year for PSA Peugeot-Citroën, with both of their 1987 new car releases impressing the European Car of the Year judges.

Of the two, it was the Peugeot 405 that took the award, scoring 464 points to beat the Citroën AX into second place by 212 votes, a margin that has never been beaten and only once equalled (in 2013, when the VW Gold topped the poll).

The ECOTY judges don't always get it right, but this time their evaluation was spot-on. The 405 was a massive hit for Peugeot, selling very well in Europe and then going on to be built in Iran, where it enjoyed a long production life.

Q8. *How many Chrysler Turbine Cars were built?*

D. 55

There was a time when the gas turbine engine – smooth, light and able to use a variety of fuels for power – was evaluated for use in cars.

Chrysler was one of those who took a particular interest in gas turbine engines, unveiling their first gas turbine car in 1954 and later undertaking the 3000 mile journey from New York to Los Angeles in a gas turbine-powered Plymouth, using both petrol and diesel as fuel. Indeed, Chrysler claimed that its engine would run on anything from peanut oil to Chanel No.5 - assuming of course that they had plentiful supplies to each to satisfy the Plymouth's 13 miles per gallon* thirst.

Chrysler continued to develop gas turbine cars, and in 1962 they announced a programme to make a small amount of gas turbine cars available to the public for real-world evaluation. And that's exactly what they did – between 1964 and 1966 a fleet of Chrysler Turbine cars were loaned to members of the public for 3 month terms. In all, just over 200 people drove the Turbine Cars for a total distance of around 1,000,000 miles.

It made for great PR but the reality was that the gas turbine engine wasn't ideally suited to cars. It was thirsty, dirty (at least in terms of the amount of nitrogen oxide it emitted), had poor throttle response, and offered no engine braking effect.

Most of the 55 Turbine Cars built were scrapped, but several continue to exist as museum pieces. Chrysler persevered with their research into gas turbines until the late 1970s, but the engine's salient problems were too deep-rooted to make it a turbine-powered road car viable.

*I assume that the reference is to US gallons, one US gallon being equivalent to 0.83 UK gallons.

Q9. *The strapline in a 1970s advert for which car stated "Takes you from 0 to the Magistrates Court in 11.4 seconds"?*

B.   Triumph Dolomite Sprint

In days of yore, car manufacturers and advertising agencies enjoyed rather more freedom than they do today, and they made full use of it.

One such printed advert, the work of the renowned Saatchi & Saatchi advertising agency, was for the Triumph Dolomite Sprint, one of the first mass-produced cars to have more than two valves per cylinder.

In the advert, a Dolomite Sprint is parked in front of a Jaguar police car. Two figures stand next to the Dolomite: its driver and a police officer who is holding a notebook. As the accompanying text explains, the Dolomite Sprint can out-accelerate not only cars which carry similar price tags but those which cost rather more to buy. And as the ad, points out, it's so quick (going from rest to an illegal (in the UK) 71 miles per hour in around 11.4 seconds) that putting your foot down too far could attract some unwelcome company...

Q10. *To the nearest thousand, how many Lancia Gammas (Berlina and Coupe) were built?*

D.   22,000

There was more to the Lancia Gamma than a pretty face, for its handsome lines played host to a flaw that was its undoing: its flat-four all-aluminium engine.

Launched in 1976, the front-wheel drive, Pininfarina-styled Gamma range was composed of two models: the Berlina, the first to appear, was a handsome four door saloon that looked a little bit like the Beta's bigger brother, and the Coupe, which appeared in

1977, was an angular two-door Coupe that looked as sharp as an Armani suit.

Both cars featured the same 2.5 litre (a 2.0 litre version was sold in Italy) flat-four engine that was unique to the model. Of all-aluminium construction, the engine was light, low and hideously unreliable. Its main problem was that it was underdeveloped and was affected by flaws which should have been eradicated before production commenced. On top of that, the power steering pump was connected to the leftmost of the Gamma's two timing belts rather than to, as was usual, the crankshaft pulley. The result of this was that when the pump was placed under strain, such as when the steering was turned to full lock, the timing belt snapped, with messy and costly consequences.

Add in a typical 1970s propensity to corrosion, and you can see why such the gorgeous Gammas struggled to find buyers. When production finally ended in 1984, just 22,062 examples (15,272 Berlinas and 6,790 Coupes) had been built.

4

GENERAL KNOWLEDGE 2

Q1. *The Hillman Hunter GLS featured an engine tuned by...?*

C. Holbay

The Hunter was six years old (and would remain on sale for a further seven) when the GLS model appeared in 1972.

As the sportiest model in the Hunter range, the specification of the GLS included four headlights, Rostyle wheels, beefed-up suspension, and a close-ratio gearbox with optional overdrive. It was, however, the engine that set it apart from lesser Hunters, having been tweaked by Holbay, a small engineering company renowned as engine tuners for road and track.

The work undertaken by Holbay included raising the compression ratio, fitting a sportier camshaft and improving engine breathing through the use of two twin-choke Weber carburettors and a 4-branch exhaust system. In this guise, the Hunter's 1725cc engine developed 93 bhp and 106 lb/ft of torque, trifling amounts by today's standards but enough to make the Hunter GLS one of the best performers in its class.

European production of the Hunter ended in 1979, but it thereafter enjoyed a very long life in Iran, where it was sold as the Paykan.

Holbay went into liquidation in 1992 but the rights to the Holbay name and other parts of its intellectual property were purchased by the son of one of the company's founders and thereafter absorbed into his own company, Dunnell Engines, which continues to operate.

Q2. *The platform of the Aston Martin DB7 was based on that of which car?*

D. Jaguar XJS

As a replacement for the E-Type, the Jaguar XJ-S (the hyphen was later dropped) didn't quite cut the mustard, although it was a fine car when considered in a different context.

In 1980, Jaguar (then part of state-owned British Leyland) embarked on the process of creating a genuine successor to the E-Type. Two cars were contemplated, a coupe (project name XJ41) and a convertible (project name XJ42). However, a number of factors, including the privatisation of Jaguar, resulted in the project being significantly delayed. So much so that the cars were still in development when Ford acquired Jaguar at the end of 1989.

Faced with a car that was too late and (by this time) too heavy, Ford pulled the plug on the programme. But although it was the end of the XJ41 and XJ42, it turned out to be the beginning of the Aston Martin DB7.

The story goes that Ian Callum, then Head of Design for Tom Walkinshaw Racing ('TWR'), a racing and engineering company which had collaborated with Jaguar on both road cars and racing programmes, was shown the defunct XJ41 and XJ42 prototypes. When Callum duly told TWR owner Tom Walkinshaw about the prototypes, Walkinshaw asked him to design a new Jaguar sports car.

A prototype was built and shown to Jaguar's top executives, only for them to reject it. As luck would have it, however, the CEO of Aston Martin was interested in the project. Callum was asked to revise the car's styling to make it look more like an Aston Martin and the project began afresh.

Due to budgetary restrictions, the new car would have to 'borrow' parts from other cars from within the Ford stable, such as the Mazda 323 and MX-5, and the Ford Scorpio. Moreover, it would use a supercharged version of the Jaguar AJ6 engine. And just to put the cherry on the cake, its chassis was based on that of the XJS, albeit with numerous alterations.

But none of this mattered, for Ian Callum had excelled himself by producing a car that was not only beautiful but looked every inch an Aston Martin, even if some naysayers refused to accept it as one.

It entered production in 1994 as the Aston Martin DB7 and enjoyed a ten year production run, during which time it easily outsold every previous Aston Martin.

Q3. *The first Tesla road car was based on which other car?*

B. Lotus Elise

In 2008, the first Tesla road car was released, a two-seat, electrically-powered roadster, the product of an agreement with Lotus.

Known simply as the Tesla Roadster, the car resembled the Lotus Elise to such an extent that to inexpert eyes it could pass as a Lotus Elise with different badges and no tailpipe. But although it looked like an Elise and had a chassis designed and built by Lotus, the Roadster shared few components with the Lotus.

The Roadster's combination of an electric motor and heavy lithium-ion battery packs meant that weighed around 50% more than an Elise, causing it to be somewhat less agile than the Lotus. Its range also lagged behind that of the Elise, particularly if its excellent performance (it was more accelerative than the Lotus) was exploited. And then there was the price – a UK market example carried a price tag starting at £86,850 in 2010.

Production ended in 2012, with 2,450 Roadsters having been built.

Q4. *What was the name of the British Rail service that transported passengers with their cars?*

D.   Motorail

Although the name *Motorail* was introduced in 1966, the concept of trains that accommodated both passengers and their cars stemmed from the Car-Sleeper Limited train that entered service between London and Perth in 1953.

The creation of the *Motorail* brand in 1966 coincided with the opening of the UK's first dedicated car train terminal at Kensington Olympia station in London. From this hub, *Motorail* services ran to several distant (from London) parts of the UK, including Penzance, Fishguard, Plymouth, Inverness and Carlisle.

Conceived at a time when there were fewer motorways, and cars were generally slower, less comfortable and less reliable, *Motorail* offered the option of being able to undertake journeys with less stress and in greater comfort. But although a mixture and daytime and overnight services were offered, *Motorail* was not a profitable venture for BR, and its popularity declined as better roads and more capable cars appeared.

Motorail services ended when BR was disaggregated and privatised in 1995, although First Great Western did run a Paddington to Penzance *Motorail* service from 1999 to 2005.

Few traces of *Motorail* now remain, one exception (at the time of writing) being the former terminal building at Kensington Olympia, which is now used as a car park.

Q5. *Bruce Forsyth appeared in a UK TV advertisement for which car?*

A.   Chrysler Avenger

Having started out as a theatre performer, Bruce Forsyth became a staple of British television for decades, enjoying particular success as a game show host.

He was arguably at the height of his fame when he appeared in a UK television commercial for the Chrysler Avenger. In the advert, Forsyth played the part of a salesman who keenly demonstrated some of the Avenger's features to a couple in a showroom, only to find that the couple had already bought the Avenger next to the one he was trying to sell them.

It's unclear whether or not the commercial, which dates from 1978, was commissioned before or after Chrysler Europe was sold to PSA that year. Like other British-market Chryslers, the Avenger became a Talbot in 1979, although it retained the Chrysler Pentastar badge on its grille until production ended in 1981.

Q6. *Stylist Chris Bangle is best known for his work with which company?*

B. BMW

Born and raised in the USA, Chris Bangle's first job in vehicle design was with Opel, for whom he worked from 1981 to 1985.

Having cut his teeth in Germany, Bangle moved on to Centro Stile Fiat where he was responsible for the striking lines of the Fiat Coupe – perhaps his best and most-loved design. He left Fiat for BMW in 1992, rising to become the first American to be appointed as the marque's Head of Design.

During his time at BMW, Bangle was primarily responsible responsible for ditching the marque's use of traditional styling cues in favour of a more radical sculpted look. The result was a series of cars with looks that were best described as polarising; if Marmite made a car then Chris Bangle would be its stylist. But like them or not, Bangle's designs were never dull.

He left BMW in 2009 to form his own design consultancy.

Q7. *At which motor show did the Mazda MX-5 make its debut?*

B. Chicago

The car that's known variously as the MX-5, Eunos, and Miata was originally the brainchild of Bob Hall, an American journalist.

It's a long story, but the gist of it is that in the late 1970s Hall suggested to Kenichi Yamomoto, who was then Mazda's Chief Engineer, that the company should think about building a small, affordable, two-seat roadster.

Nothing came of it at the time, but Hall's suggestion had made an impact. So much so that a couple of years later, Hall (who was by then working for Mazda in California) was given the green light to do some initial work – in his spare time – on his suggested two-seat roadster.

The project was given a boost when Mark Jordan joined the Mazda design team in California, and it was his clay model (which looks like a slightly larger version of the car that went into production) which was presented to the Mazda board.

Although board approval was given, it It would be several years before the production version of the MX-5 was ready. But when that moment arrived, the MX-5 made its public debut in the land in which it had first been conceived.

Q8. *The Bellini sports car in the 1960 film 'School for Scoundrels' was really a disguised...?*

C. Aston Martin DB3S

Aside from being a very funny film, *School for Scoundrels* offers a few treats for petrolheads, with the film's hero acquiring first a '1924 Swiftmobile' (a disguised Bentley 4½ litre), to great comedic effect, and later an Austin Healey 100/6.

The vehicular star of the film is, however, the car owned by the hero's caddish antagonist, brilliantly portrayed by Terry-Thomas. Referred to in the film as a Bellini, in reality it's a disguised Aston Martin DB3S, one of five built.

Used by Aston Martin owner David Brown as his personal road car, the DB3S which appears in the film was also pressed into service by the works Aston Martin racing team. It was raced in period by Stirling Moss, Tony Brooks, Peter Collins, Graham Hill, Roy Salvadori, and Reg Parnell.

Having passed into private ownership, the DB3S continued to compete, with tragic consequences. In 1958, a young mechanic named Alan Overton drove it in the Gosport Motor Club Speed Trials in Portsmouth. Having passed the finish line, Overton failed to apply the car's brakes, with the result that both car and driver ended up in Langstone Harbour. Although the car was recovered and later rebuilt, Overton did not survive the crash.

In 2016, Bonhams offered the DB3S at auction. It was expected to realise a sale price of between £6,000,000 and £7,000,000, but did not sell.

Q9. *As of 2021, the title of European Car of the Year has never been awarded to a car built by...?*

A. **BMW**

Believe it or not, as of 2021 no BMW car has ever awarded the title of European Car of the Year. That gives the marque a unique distinction among mainstream German car manufacturers, with Audi, Mercedes-Benz, Volkswagen, Porsche and even NSU each having produced at least one recipient of the accolade.

And to perhaps add injury to insult, BMW cars have only finished second in the ECOTY voting on four occasions in the award's history, those cars being the 1600 in 1967, the 3 Series (E21) in 1976, the 7 Series (E23) in 1978, and the i3 in 2014.

Q10. *Nigel Mansell and Tiff Needell raced in British Formula 3 in cars powered by which engine?*

A.   Triumph 2.0 litre 16 valve slant-four

They never raced together as team-mates but both Nigel Mansell and Tiff Needell raced Unipart-sponsored March cars with Triumph engines in the British Formula 3 championships.

Having made its F3 debut in 1976, the Triumph engine powered the March F3 cars of Tiff Needell and Ian Taylor in 1977 and 1978. They found the going tough, with Taylor's victory at Silverstone in 1977 being the team's sole success in those two years.

For 1979, the team was represented by Nigel Mansell and Brett Riley, but results remained hard to come by, with Mansell and Riley winning one race apiece.

The Unipart sponsorship and the Triumph engines disappeared from F3 after the 1980 season. As no other teams had used Triumph power, the three victories taken by the Unipart cars from 1977 to 1979 were the engine's only race wins in the British F3 championships.

Save for around 60 pre-production Triumph TR7 Sprints, the roadgoing version of the Triumph slant-four 16 valve engine was only used in a single car, the Triumph Dolomite Sprint.

5

MOTORSPORT

Q1. Which car took victory in the 1970 London to Mexico Rally?

C. Ford Escort

Following on from England's victory in the 1966 football World Cup and the success of the 1968 London to Sydney Marathon, running a rally from London, venue of the 1966 World Cup final, to Mexico City, where the 1970 final would be held, must have seemed like a good idea.

With sponsorship from the *Daily Mail*, the rally attracted over 100 entries from both manufacturers and privateers. Ford and British Leyland took a particular interest in it, the former running several Escort mark 1s with 1850cc Kent engines whilst BL entered a three car team of Triumph 2500 Pi saloons and a second team equipped with Maxis, Austin 1800s and a Mini Cooper S. Citroën entered several DS21s and even the USSR got in on the act, with Avtoexport fielding no fewer than 5 Moskvich 412s. Other cars to take part the rally included two Rolls Royces, Porsche 911s, a Trident Venturer V6, and a Volkswagen Buggy.

The entry list included several top-line rally drivers, including Hannu Mikkola, Roger Clark, Timo Makinen, Tony Fall, Rauno Aaltonen, Brian Culcheth and Andrew Cowan. Other notable entrants were footballer Jimmy Greaves and Prince Michael of Kent.

The rally started in London and took in several European countries before those competitors who were still running flew from Portugal to Brazil. From there, the rally wound its way through South and Central America (including another journey by air), finally ending in Mexico

City a little over five weeks after leaving London.

It was a tough, gruelling contest and only 26 of the 106 starters were classified as finishers. The list of finishers included Citroen driver Henri Marang, who was killed in an accident three days before the end of the rally.

Ford took the victory courtesy of Hannu Mikkola and Gunnar Palm, with Brian Culcheth and Johnstone Syer taking second place for BL. Jimmy Greaves partnered Tony Fall to sixth place in an Escort. He fared better than Prince Michael of Kent, who made to Brazil but crashed out of the rally shortly after leaving Rio De Janeiro.

Q2. *Which of the following cars NEVER won the overall British Saloon Car Championship?*

A. Ford Capri 3000S

If you watched the British Saloon Car Championship in the late 1970s and early 1980s then you'd have been accustomed to the sight of a gaggle of Capris battling out for outright race wins. But although the Capri took the lion's share of outright victories, the overall championship was decided on the basis of a driver's results against other cars in his or her class. This meant that the overall champion invariably came from one of the less hotly contested classes than the class in which the Capri competed.

Thus it was that Capri driver Gordon Spice took more outright race wins than any other driver over a period of several years but never placed higher than third in the overall championship.

Q3. *Which tuning expert managed Dealer Team Vauxhall's racing and rallying programme?*

B.   Bill Blydenstein

In days of yore, the individuals who ran racing and/or rally teams on behalf of car manufacturers were household names – well, at least in so far as petrolheads were concerned.

This was certainly true of Bill Blydenstein, a Dutch-born tuning expert under whose guidance Dealer Team Vauxhall ('DTV') enjoyed considerable success in racing, particularly with the exuberant Gerry Marshall as a driver.

Blydenstein later also took charge of DTV's rallying programme, the highlight of his tenure being in 1979 when Pentti Airikkala won the British Rallying Championship for Vauxhall – a significant achievement given that the series was then contested by some of the finest rally drivers in the world.

Q4. *What car did F1 and Indy Car champion Nigel Mansell drive in the 1993 TOCA Shootout?*

D.   Ford Mondeo

It was quite a coup for the organisers to entice Nigel Mansell to race in the TOCA Shootout, a non-championship race held at Donington Park in October 1993. Mansell was, after all, both the reigning F1 World Champion and the Indy Car World Series Champion. Indeed he remains to this day the only driver ever to have simultaneously held both titles, albeit only for a few weeks.

His steed for the race was a works Ford Mondeo Si, a car that had scored three late-season wins in the BTCC championship in the hands of Paul Radisich. Mansell's presence notwithstanding, the entry list for the Shootout was somewhat more anaemic than for a regular season BTCC race, with several teams and drivers giving it a miss. That said, Mansell's box-office appeal saw 60,000 people attend the meeting,

The race itself was eventful. Having been fifth fastest in practice, he was running third in the race when he lost control at the Old Hairpin, tangled with Tiff Needell's Vauxhall and slammed into a concrete wall at considerable speed. He was knocked out in the crash and spent a night in hospital.

Mansell returned to touring cars in 1998, when he drove a Mondeo in three rounds of the British Touring Car Championship, scoring a best result of fifth in a wet race at Donington Park.

Q5. *1976 F1 World Champion James Hunt later owned a van based on which car?*

A. Austin A35

As a driver, James Hunt's colourful off-track antics attracted as many column inches as his racing successes.

Having retired from motorsport during the 1979 F1 season at the young age of 31, Hunt went on to forge a second career as a witty and sometimes pithy member of the BBC's F1 commentary team. But it wasn't all roses for the erstwhile champion. He lost a considerable amount of money, having invested in a number of insurance syndicates at Lloyd's, and his second marriage failed.

In his later years, he lived in Wimbledon in a large house that was also home to his German Shepherd, his foul-mouthed parrot, and his show budgerigars. His usual form of motor transport, an Austin A35 van, sat on his driveway, alongside his 6.9 litre Mercedes 450 SEL, which sat immobile on bricks due to his straitened financial circumstances.

It was old, slow and noisy, but Hunt loved his A35 van, reckoning it to be the ideal form of transport in which to transport his budgies to and from shows.

Somehow I just can't see any of today's F1 stars following suit. But then James Hunt really was a one-off.

Q6. *Which F1 driver later worked for Lotus Engineering and played an important role in the development of several road cars for both Lotus and its clients?*

C. John Miles

John Miles started 12 Grands Prix, all of them for Lotus. In 1969, as the team's third driver he was largely responsible for testing the team's new four-wheel drive Lotus 63. He raced the slow, heavy and complicated 63 in five Grands Prix that season but only finished once, when he took 10th place at Silverstone.

His efforts were rewarded with a full-time drive for Lotus in 1970, where he partnered Jochen Rindt. But whilst Rindt scored a series of victories, Miles was well off the pace. His only points finish in F1 came at the South African Grand Prix, where he finished a lapped fifth.

Having parted company with Team Lotus after Rindt's death at Monza, Miles moved to BRM for 1971. He mostly served as the team's test driver but competed in two non-championship races, his last as an F1 driver.

Although Miles was not successful in F1, he was a highly accomplished sports car racer. He also showed up well in F3 and on his few outings in F2. His called a halt to his racing career in 1972, having teamed up with Brian Muir to win the Paul Ricard 6 Hours in a Capri RS2600, leading home the works Capris of Jackie Stewart/Francois Cevert and Gerard Larrousee/Alex Soler-Roig/Jochen Mass.

Miles then went on to forge successful careers as an engineer and motoring journalist. In his latter capacity, his well-judged observations graced the pages of *Autocar* magazine, and as an engineer he worked for Lotus Engineering on a number of projects, both for Lotus and other manufacturers. These included the Lotus Sunbeam, the Elan M100 and the first generation Ford Focus. He was involved with Lotus' work on active suspension and even made a brief return to Team Lotus. After 18 years with Lotus Engineering,

Miles then spent a further three with Aston Martin.

That's quite a CV, but there's more, including doing some of the driving in the Steve McQueen film *Le Mans*, plus co-founding a record label devoted to jazz music.

Q7. *How many BTCC race wins were scored by the Volvo 850 Estate?*

B. None

There was a time when motor manufacturers played a very active role in the BTCC, hiring the best teams and drivers and spending a pretty penny or two in the pursuit of success. It was a philosophy born out of the old adage, "Win on Sunday, sell on Monday."

Indeed, by 1994 no fewer than ten manufacturers fielded teams in the BTCC: Ford, Vauxhall, Mazda, Peugeot, Renault, BMW, Toyota, Nissan, Alfa Romeo, and Volvo. Heady days indeed.

For their BTCC debut, Volvo had joined forces with Tom Walkinshaw Racing to campaign the Volvo 850. Correction, make that the Volvo 850 Estate. One wonders what drivers Jan Lammers, who had raced in F1 and won Le Mans, and Rickard Rydell, a race winner in Formula 3, thought of it.

In the face of strong competition, the big Volvo struggled to make much of an impression in terms of results. No wins or podium finishes came its way, its best race results being a pair of fifth places, one each for Lammers and Rydell.

This lack of results did not deter Volvo, who returned the following year with the 850 saloon, scoring six race victories. More wins for the 850 came in 1996 but the introduction of a new car to the BTCC in 1997, the S40 saloon, was marked only by a single win.

It finally all came good for Volvo in 1998, when Rydell notched five race wins on his way to the Driver's Championship. He scored several more wins for Volvo in 1999, but had to settle for third in the standings. That was Volvo's final season in the BTCC.

In recent years, estate cars have made a return to the BTCC in the form of the Honda Civic Tourer in 2014 and the Subaru Levorg from 2016 to 2019. The Honda proved good enough to take four race wins but the Subaru fared even better, notching 21 race wins and the 2017 Driver's championship for Ash Sutton.

But here's an odd thing. Ask any longtime fan of the BTCC to name their favourite estate car from the series and the chances are that they'll choose the one that never won a race: the 850. Sometimes being the first can be make a bigger impression than coming first.

Q8. *In which car did Formula 1 team managers compete for the Jack Brabham Trophy in 1971?*

B. Ford Escort Mexico

It's very, very hard to imagine that a race involving Formula 1 team principals in identical cars could ever happen. But in October 1971, that's exactly what did happen.

The race took place at Brands Hatch on the weekend that it hosted the end of season Rothmans World Championship Victory Race, a non-championship race run to Formula One rules. As ever, though, the main race was supported by a number of other contests, including what was to be the only running of the Jack Brabham Trophy to ever take place.

Amongst the 15 competitors were several F1 team principals: Colin Chapman of Lotus, Ken Tyrrell, John Surtees, Alan Rees of March, Phil Kerr of McLaren, Frank Williams, and Tim Parnell of BRM. They were joined by Jack Brabham himself, Mike Costin of Cosworth, Max Mosley (the commercial supremo and co-owner of March), Eric Broadley (founder and chief designer of Lola Cars), Jackie Epstein, Doug Hardwick, Ed Nelson, and Ian Williams.

Each competitor was allocated a Ford Escort Mexico that had been prepared by Ford's Advanced Vehicle Operation in Essex. In theory, therefore, the cars were identical, although Lotus engineer Tony Rudd was seen to spend about 20 minutes with his head under the bonnet of Chapman's car!

The race itself took place over 10 laps of the Brands Hatch Club Circuit (now known as the Indy Circuit). Having been fastest in practice, Brabham started from pole position ahead of Chapman, Surtees, Mosley et. al.

Brabham led from the start and spent most of the race at the head of the field. On the final lap, however, Chapman passed him for the lead and established what seemed to be a race-winning margin. However, Chapman suffered gear selection problems as he came round the final corner, enabling first Brabham and then Surtees to pass him. Brabham thus took the win* but sportingly gave Chapman the winner's trophy.

The race was televised, with Graham Hill joining Barrie Gill on commentary duties. It's available on You Tube and is well worth watching, both for the racing and for Hill's witty observations.

*As an aside, Brabham's win came the year after he lost certain victory in the British Grand Prix at Brands Hatch due to running out of fuel on the final corner.

Q9. *What was the MG Metro 6R4's best result in a round of the World Rally Championship?*

A. Third

The foundations of the Metro 6R4 project were laid down in 1980, when BL retired the Triumph TR7 V8 from international competition and set about the task of building a car that would challenge for victory in the World Rally Championship.

To help them achieve this goal, BL approached Williams Grand

Prix Engineering and an agreement was reached whereby BL would supervise the project and build the new car's engine, whilst Williams would take care of designing and building the prototype.

The first fruits of Williams' involvement were quickly realised when Patrick Head of Williams suggested to BL that they should abandon their plans for a front-engined car and instead go for a mid-engined configuration.

Whilst work on the car proceeded, Austin Rover's engineers were hard at work on a new engine for it. That would take time to realise but in the meantime two cylinders were lopped off the trusty Rover V8, thus creating a six-cylinder engine that was small enough to fit into the Metro's compact bodyshell.

It was in this guise that the first prototype was tested by rally ace Tony Pond in February 1983. Two further prototypes were shortly thereafter handed over by Williams, leaving the project now solely in the hands of Austin Rover. For the rest of that year, the 6R4 was tested at a variety of venues whilst work continued on the engine that would ultimately power it.

The following year, the 6R4's public launch took place at Heathrow Airport. A few weeks later, it contested a rally – the York National – for the first time. It made a splash by establishing a comfortable lead before retiring due to an alternator fire. It thereafter entered several more rallies, which served as useful test and development mileage as the team finalised it for homologation into Group B.

By the start of 1985, the 6R4 had considerably evolved from the first prototype. The new engine was not, however, quite ready, so the stop-gap V62V engine continued to be used. And it was this unit that powered the 6R4 to its first rally victory - Tony Pond and co-driver Rob Arthur winning the Skip Brown Rally by a margin of just under two minutes.

That was the last rally in which the V62V engine featured. Henceforth the 6R4 would be equipped with the new V64V engine in either international or less powerful 'clubman' specification.

Now that the new engine was ready, the 6R4 was now offered to customers in order to satisfy Group B homologation requirements. To avoid the need for Type Approval, it was sold in kit form, which in reality meant that it only needed a few components to fitted in order to be useable.

Further victories for the 6R4 followed, with Pond and Arthur winning the Autofit Argyle Stages, and Ken Wood taking the first victory for a 'customer' 6R4 on the Sprint Tyres Trossachs Rally, two days after taking delivery of it!

The 6R4 made its World Rally Championship debut on the 1985 Lombard RAC Rally. It did well, Pond and Arthur bringing it home in third place, but it was no match for the new Lancia Delta S4s of Toivonen and Alen. Nor would it ever be – Austin Rover had elected to plump for a normally aspirated engine for the 6R4, reasoning that it would be more reliable than a turbocharged unit. Unfortunately, it was simply outgunned by the turbocharged opposition (the Delta S4 was both turbocharged and supercharged), and in a WRC season that saw both tragedy and controversy, the 6R4's best finish was fourth place on the San Remo Rally.

Following the FIA's decision to scrap Group B with effect from the end of the 1986 season, Austin Rover withdrew from rallying. The 6R4 continued, however, to be used in national rallies throughout the British Isles, being popular with both drivers and spectators.

As for the V64V engine, it was further developed by Tom Walkinshaw Racing and went to to power the Jaguar XJ220 supercar – ironically, in turbocharged form.

Q10. *Henri Toivonen drove which car to second place in the 1978 Arctic Rally?*

D.   Chrysler Avenger

For a car that, let's face it, really wasn't very sporty, the Chrysler Avenger actually did fairly well in motorsport.

In the hands of Bernard Unett, the Avenger took three outright victories in the British Saloon Car Championship. It was no slouch as a rally car either, with Andrew Cowan winning the 1976 New Zealand Rally, and Robin Eyre-Maunsell winning the Group 1 British Rally Championship in both 1975 and 1976. Moreover, Scott Harvey won the 1971 Press on Regardless Rally in the USA at the wheel of a Plymouth Cricket, a British-built, badge-engineered version of the Avenger for the American market.

That said, the Avenger's finest hour as a rally car arguably came in 1978, when Henri Toivonen drove one to second place in the Arctic Rally, beating Markku Alen's Fiat 131 Abarth into third place, and that in the year that Alen won the FIA Cup for Drivers (the precursor of the World Championship). Moreover, Avengers also came home in fifth and seventh places.

Toivonen would go on to become (at the time) the youngest ever winner of a World Championship rally. Appropriately enough, this would come at the wheel of the Avenger's hatchback cousin, the Sunbeam.

IT PAYS TO ADVERTISE 6

Q1. *The products of which car company were promoted on UK television by The Two Ronnies?*

B. British Leyland

Humour is a great means of getting just about any message across, so it's no surprise that TV advertisers have long used comedy as a means of selling their products.

In the late 1970s and early 1980s, two of Britain's best-loved funny men, Ronnie Barker and Ronnie Corbett, starred in commercials promoting British Leyland products. To all intents and purposes the commercials shared the same sharp, witty and character-driven recipe as a typical Two Ronnies comedy sketch. If only the cars had been as good as the commercials...

As an aside, the Two Ronnies also appeared in Hertz commercials in the 1980s. Like the BL ads, they can be found on You Tube.

Q2. *Nicole and Papa were characters in UK television adverts for which car?*

D. Renault Clio

The characters of Nicole and Papa, respectively played by Estelle Skornik and Max Douchin, first appeared on UK TV screens in 1991. It has been claimed that Skornik didn't actually have a driving licence at the time that first commercial was filmed, a rumour that was subsequently scotched by the actress herself.

The advertisements were hugely successful, to the extent that Nicole and Papa became staples of British TV advertising until their final appearance in 1998, when they were joined by Vic Reeves and Bob Mortimer in a commercial that took its storyline from the ending of the 1967 film, *The Graduate*. Oh, and if you're wondering, Bob got the girl.

It's perhaps also worth noting that one 1996 survey reported that Nicole was recognised by more Britons that Chris Evans, Bob Hoskins, and the then Prime Minister, John Major.

Q3. ***A song by which musical artist was used in UK television advertising for the Peugeot 206?***

B. Lenny Kravitz

With the 206, Peugeot almost* achieved the remarkable feat of supplanting its much-loved and hugely successful 205 supermini in the hearts and minds of the public.

The 206 was undeniably an attractive car but Peugeot was, at least at first, content to base their advertising on the sense of freedom that it offered rather than the way it looked. That being so, Lenny Kravitz's 'Fly Away' with its yearning for escape and freedom to explore made for an ideal soundtrack.

The campaign was a huge success for both Peugeot and Kravitz, with the 206 becoming a roaring success throughout Europe, and 'Fly Away' giving Kravitz his first and so far only UK number 1 single.

*I say 'almost' because no small Peugeot has yet managed to oust the sportier 205s, such as the Rallye and GTI, from the hearts of petrolheads.

Q4. *Which French sports car was advertised using a slogan which translates as "The teeth of the road"?*

B.   Talbot-Matra Murena

An odd but memorable slogan. The thinking behind this one was probably that since (for reasons best known to Matra) the Murena was named after a type of moray eel, it made sense to incorporate a reference to teeth into the advertising campaign. Given, however, that sales of the Murena were much lower than that of its predecessor, the Matra-Simca Bagheera, one might suggest that the advert lacked bite!

And just in case you're wondering, the original French advert read: "Murena. Les dents de la route."

Q5. *Which American actor appeared in the 'New Rules' TV advertisements for the Vauxhall Vectra in 2002?*

D.   Ed Harris

The third and final incarnation of the Vauxhall Vectra was launched in 2002. To emphasise its feature set, a scenario was dreamed up in which Vauxhall was going to court to seek what was in effect a legal declarator that the car was loaded with innovations.

The story took place over a series of three television adverts, in all of which renowned American actor Ed Harris played a lawyer tasked with presenting the case for the Vectra.

In the first advert, Harris embarked on an information-gathering exercise in order to prepare his case. The focus thereafter switched to him examining witnesses in court and addressing a jury about some of the Vectra's new features, which he said made it "a phenomenon".

And in the final advert – you know where this is going, don't you – Harris emerged triumphant from the court. He climbed into the passenger seat of a Vectra, and as the car drove away, a news announcer on the car's radio stated that "In a landmark court ruling, it was proven that the Vectra sets new rules in the car industry."

Q6. *Which song was used in early UK television commercials for the Renault 21?*

A.   I Feel Free

Originally performed by Cream (Eric Clapton, Jack Bruce, and Ginger Baker), I Feel Free was released as a single in 1966, reaching its highest position of number 11 in the UK Singles Chart in January 1967.

Nearly two decades later, the UK TV advertisement for the newly-launched Renault 21 featured a new version of the track, re-recorded by Jack Bruce. It was rather less successful, reaching number 95, but nonetheless gave Bruce his only solo entry in the UK Singles Chart.

Q7. *Who appeared in a UK TV commercial for the Chrysler Alpine and later went on to present 'Top Gear'?*

C.   William Woollard

William Woollard first came to the public's attention as a presenter on the BBC science and technology programme, *Tomorrow's World*.

In 1978, the same year in which he left *Tomorrow's World*, Woollard appeared in a TV commercial for the Chrysler Alpine. Given Woollard was a reputable presenter of science and fact-based television, he was no doubt thought to be the ideal person to persuade the British public that the Alpine's hatchback configuration made it an ideal family car, and that its relatively small engines were at least as capable as the larger capacity units employed by its competitors.

Alas, the commercial didn't quite have the desired impact, and UK sales of the Alpine continued to decline after a promising start. It did no harm to Woollard's career, however, as he subsequently spent a decade as a presenter on the *Top Gear* motoring programme whilst also presenting *Rally Report*, the BBC's annual show covering the running of the RAC Rally.

Q8. *What car was advertised with the slogan "In and out like Ronald Biggs..."*

D.   Mini

Believe it or not, a printed advert for the Mini once used the strapline "In and out like Ronald Biggs."

At the time that the advert was used, Biggs was a fugitive from justice, having escaped from H.M. Prison Wandsworth where he was serving a sentence of imprisonment for his part in The Great Train Robbery, in which £2.6 million was stolen from the Glasgow – London mail train.

Accordingly, the advert could have referred to the robbery itself, Biggs' imprisonment and subsequent escape, or both.

Q9. *An aria from which opera was used in the UK television advert for the Fiat Strada?*

A.   The Barber of Seville

If you're of a certain age, you'll probably remember the Fiat Strada '*Handbuilt by robots*' TV commercial. It made a big enough impact at the time for the *Not The Nine O'Clock News* team to not only lampoon it in their '*Driven by Italians*' sketch but also to pay homage to it a couple of years later in their Austin Ambassador '*Handbuilt by Roberts*' sketch.

As for the music in the commercial, it's Figaro's Aria from Rossini's opera, *The Barber of Seville*. At the time of writing, you can find the original commercial plus the aforementioned *Not the Nine O'Clock News* sketches on You Tube. All are well worth checking out.

Q10. ***According to its makers' advertising, what car was "The shape of things to come"?***

C.   Triumph TR7

Well, that's what Triumph said anyway!

A rather different opinion was said to have been offered by design maestro Giorgetto Giugiaro when he first saw the TR7 coupé. Having walked round the car, Giugiaro allegedly exclaimed, "My God! They've done it to the other side as well!" Whilst that may well be an apocryphal story, it's simply too good not to mention.

In fairness, the TR7 has dated well, and the drophead version has always been a fine looking car. It could also be said that the TR7, whilst not the first wedge-shaped car, was at least one of the earlier ones, which does give at least some credence to its makers' claim.

Q1. *To the nearest thousand, how many examples of the Talbot Tagora were built?*

A. 20,000

The Tagora is one of the forgotten cars of the 1980s.

Intended as a replacement for the aged Chrysler 160/180/2 litre range, the Tagora (or C9, to use its makers' designation) was styled in the UK and developed in France. With the mid-1970s energy crisis over, Chrysler Europe had high hopes for the C9, and their Executive Director of Product Development boldly forecast annual sales of 60,000 cars. Of course, that's not how it turned out.

When PSA acquired Chrysler Europe in 1978, they decided to press on with the C9 programme in spite of already having the Peugeot 604 and Citroën CX already vying for market share in the same market sector that the C9 would occupy.

PSA made several changes to the C9's design, one of which was to enable it to accept the 2.7 litre PRV V6 engine. This was to the C9's benefit, but the same could not be said about one of PSA's other changes – the decision to equip it with the same rear axle as the Peugeot 505. The result of this was to give the C9 a narrower track than had originally been intended, which adversely affected both its appearance and handling.

But even without the narrower track, the C9's appearance was problematic – it looked like a scaled-up version of the smaller and cheaper Solara saloon, something that was unlikely to find favour with buyers of executive cars.

At its launch in 1981, the Tagora was, at best, damned with faint praise. It sold slowly from the get-go, and its slim chance of attaining any semblance of respectability on the sales charts was wiped out by the recession into which it was born. Still, at least PSA didn't allow it to wither on the vine: production ended in 1983 after a total of 19,389 Tagoras had been built.

Q2. *Maurice Gatsonides, inventor of the Gatso speed camera, won which notable motorsport event?*

B.   Monte Carlo Rally

Born in 1911 in what was the then the Dutch East Indies and is now Indonesia, Maurice Gatsonides had a quite remarkable life.

Having joined Dutch airline KLM, he qualified as a flight engineer but left the company in 1935 to start his own motor business. In 1936, he competed in the Monte Carlo Rally.

He led a double life during the Second World War. On one hand, he was engaged in the production of charcoal gas generators as a means of propulsion for cars and trucks, and on the other he was active in the Dutch Resistance, helping downed airmen and escaped prisoners of war.

When the war was over, Gatsonides returned to the motor business – at one stage even attempting to put his own car into production – and rallying. He won the Monte Carlo Rally in 1953 and enjoyed a number of lesser successes before retiring from competition in the 1960s.

It was through rallying that he invented a device – the Gatsometer - that measured the time taken to travel between two fixed points. Its potential as a means of enforcing speed limits was obvious to Gatsonides, and it soon became the bane of speeding motorists.

It was followed by another of Gatsonides's creations – the speed camera – which was introduced in the 1960s but became a particularly powerful enforcement tool when later combined with radar.

Ironically, Gatsonides himself fell foul of his own inventions on a number of occasions!

Q3. *Badged as a Lancia in many markets, what badge did the Y10 supermini sport in its home market?*

C. Autobianchi

Created in 1955 as a joint venture by Fiat, Pirelli and Bianchi (then a manufacturer of bicycles and motorcycles), Autobianchi is perhaps best remembered for the A112. Introduced in 1969, the A112 was a small three-door hatchback based on a modified Fiat 128 platform.

The A112 underwent a number of revisions through its 17 year production life, including the introduction of an Abarth version. It was sold exclusively as an Autobianchi until the early 1980s, when it started to be badged as a Lancia (Fiat had taken control of Autobianchi in 1969) in some markets.

A new car, the small, stumpy and aerodynamic (its drag factor was 0.31) Autobianchi Y10, was introduced in 1985. The Y10 was produced over three generations and was sold as an Autobianchi in some markets, including Italy, and as a Lancia in others. Its range included, at various times, a sporty Turbo version and a four-wheel drive model.

Y10 production ended in 1995, and with it went the Autobianchi name.

Q4. *The Volkswagen Type 181 is known in the USA as the Volkswagen...?*

C. Thing

Originally designed for the (West) German army and launched in 1968, the Type 181 is a rear-engined, open-topped utility vehicle with four doors and a windscreen that could be folded flat. In spite of its looks - its simple, utilitarian lines were very similar to those of the *Kübelwagen*, which saw extensive service with the German military in World War 2 – the Type 181 was a modern vehicle which used the same mechanical components as the Beetle and shared its floorplan with the Karmann Ghia.

As was common with similar vehicles, such as the Citroën Mehari and the Mini Moke, the Type 181 (the RHD version was known as the Type 182) had a somewhat spartan interior, with vinyl seats, painted metal instead of plastic, drain holes in its floorpan and perforated rubber mats rather than carpets.

The first Type 181s were produced for the military but civilian sales began in continental Europe and Mexico in 1971. It was launched in the USA the following year and was briefly sold in the UK in 1975.

But although it was the same car, the Type 181 had several different names. It was sold as the *Kurierwagen* in West Germany; the Pescaccia in Italy; the *Safari* in Mexico; and the *Trekker* in the UK.

In the USA, however, it was marketed as the *Thing*, a curious name that seemed not to hinder its sales; for although it was only sold in the USA for two years (VW withdrew it from sale as it would have been unable to comply with new safety regulations) it proved popular with young people and around 25,000 were imported.

The last civilian Type 181s were produced in 1980, but the simplicity of its construction and a ready supply of mechanical components has seen many examples continue to give service as reliable, quirky looking fun cars to the present day.

Q5. *The Hofstetter Turbo sports car was built in which country?*

A. Brazil

It may have had a German-sounding name and use Volkswagen running gear but the Hofstetter Turbo was Brazil's answer to not only the Lotus Esprit but also the DeLorean DMC-12.

Its designer, Mario Richard Hofstetten, had taken his inspiration from concept cars of the 1970s. And it showed – his creation was, at least in some respects, rather like the sports car equivalent of a greatest hits package. It was low, wedge-shaped and had both pop-up headlamps and gull-wing doors. That said, its styling didn't quite jell, and it caught the eye in much the same way as might a car created by the props department for use in a 1980s sci-fi movie.

There was nothing too much wrong with its interior, nor with its mid-engined drivetrain layout. Its suspension did, however, betray the low-budget, low-volume nature of its construction; rather than a bespoke layout, the Hofstetter used the front suspension from the Chevrolet Chevette, and its rear suspension was the front suspension of the VW Passat, mounted back to front. Mind you, it wasn't the only mid-engined car of the 1980s to use saloon suspension mounted backwards – the Pontiac Fiero did likewise until its last year of production.

Power came from four-cylinder VW engines, with the first prototype being equipped with a 1.6 litre engine mated to a four-speed gearbox. Subsequent models received turbocharged VW engines of 1.8 litre and, later, 2.0 litre capacities.

It was first shown at the 1984 Brazilian Motor Show, attracting much attention. Its maker said that deliveries would begin in 1986 and around 30 would be built each year. But – and please do stop me if you've heard this one before – that's not how it worked out. For although it remained available until the early 1990s, fewer than 20 were built, in spite of later revisions that added an opening slot on the passenger window (its windows were, like those of the DMC-12, non-opening), a rear aerofoil and the option of automatic transmission.

Still, it made it into production, and that's most definitely not to be scoffed at.

Q6. ***Which of the following Renault models lacked a Gordini version in its model range?***

B. 16

Born in 1899, Amédée Gordini was an Italian racing car driver and engineer who moved to France in his 20s. There, he struck up a friendship with a fellow Italian expatriate, Henri Pigozzi, the founder of Simca.

With Pigozzi as a friend, and having established himself both as a talented racing driver and engineer, it was perhaps inevitable that Gordini would work closely with Simca on on both road and racing cars.

Having established an enviable reputation as a tuning wizard ('le sorcier') who could extract more performance from an engine without spending lavishly, Gordini set up the Gordini racing team in 1952 and achieved considerable success in Formula 2 racing. Indeed, his exploits resulted in him being awarded the Legion of Honour by the French government in 1953.

In 1957, Renault engaged Gordini's services to help them develop performance versions of their road cars. The result was Gordini versions of the *Dauphine*, *Renault 8* and *Renault 10*.

When Gordini retired in 1968, Renault bought 70% of his company from him, quickly assimilating it as Renault's sporting arm. This was followed by the creation of more Gordini-badged Renaults, with the 5, 12, and 17 ranges all including Gordini versions. Not every car built by Renault included a Gordini version, however, with those to miss out including the Renault 4, Renault 14 and Renault 16.

Q7. *What was the first name of Lord Stokes, chairman of British Leyland from 1968 to 1975?*

B. Donald

Donald Stokes was born in Plymouth in 1914.

At the age of 16, he took up an engineering apprentice with Leyland, as part of which he studied engineering at the Harris Institute of Technology in Preston. He stayed with Leyland after completing his apprenticeship, albeit his employment with them came to a temporary halt during the Second World War.

Once hostilities ended, Stokes, whose role was more that of a salesman than an engineer, played a key role in Leyland's successful export drive. Consequently, he rose through the ranks until, in 1963, he was appointed managing director of Leyland, which by this time had absorbed Standard-Triumph.

He had also become a favourite of Harold Wilson, who served as Prime Minister from 1964 to 1970. Under the Wilson regime, Stokes was placed in charge of UK arms sales and knighted. In 1968, Leyland merged with their main British rivals, BMC, to form British Leyland Motor Corporation.

Stokes was appointed as Managing Director and Deputy Chairman of the new company, whose products accounted for over 40% of the cars sold in the UK. On the face of it, it looked like a great opportunity. In reality, it was a poison chalice.

BLMC was bloated, inefficient, beset by industrial unrest, in need of investment, and was starting to see its market share fall in the face of strong competition. Stokes, who became Chairman of BLMC in 1973, did his best, but the task of stabilising and revitalising BLMC at that point in time was probably beyond the ability of any human.

At the tail end of 1974, the situation at BLMC became so dire that Stokes approached the UK government, once more headed by Wilson, for financial assistance. The government commissioned

Don Ryder to produce a report, as a consequence of which BLMC was effectively nationalised and a new holding company, British Leyland Limited, was set up.

Stokes was appointed to the BL board as its non-executive President, but in reality, he had very little influence over the company's affairs. He remained on the BL board until 1979, after which he gradually faded from the public eye.

He died in 2008, aged 94.

Q8. *Where was Bond Cars' factory situated?*

A. **Preston**

The first Bond car, the single-cylinder, three-wheeler Minicar, was launched in 1949. Although badged as a Bond, it was a product of Sharps Commercials Limited, a company which had hitherto been known as a vehicle retailer rather than a manufacturer.

The Minicar enjoyed a long production life, during which van, estate and convertible versions were added to the range.

In 1963, Bond added a four-wheel car to its roster: the Equipe. It was two-seat coupé with an attractive and sporty fibreglass body which sat on a Triumph Herald chassis and used the Herald's 1124cc engine for motive power. At around the same time, Sharp's Commercials Limited became Bond Cars Limited. r

In 1965, Bond introduced the 875, a three-wheeler that used a rear-mounted 875cc engine from the Hillman Imp. A van version, the Ranger, followed in 1967, with a mark 2 version of the 875 coming along in 1968.

The 875 was light, thanks to a fibreglass bodyshell and aluminium doors, and was both quicker and had better fuel consumption than a Mini 850. It was, however, a little more expensive than the Mini.

The final 'proper' Bond was the Equipe 2 litre, which featured a restyled bodyshell on top of the chassis and 2.0 litre six-cylinder engine from the Triumph Vitesse. It was initially offered in hard-top form but a convertible version was added to the range in 1968.

In February, 1969, Bond was acquired by a rival manufacturer of three and four wheel cars, Reliant. Production of the Equipe and 875 continued at Bond's Preston factory into 1970, and a new model - the three-wheel Bond Bug, which used Reliant running gear - was released.

By the summer of 1970, however, production of the Equipe and 875 had ended, and the Bug was now being built solely at Reliant's own factory in Tamworth. With the spare parts business for the Minicar, 875 and Equipe having been sold to an Oldbury-based company, this spelled the end of the road for the former Bond factory in Preston.

It shut in December of that year, and only part of the external wall of it now remains.

Q9. *Which of the following pop stars once worked at a car factory?*

D.   Bob Marley

There's a well-known photograph of a young man installing a Mini rear window on a production line. That young man looks for all the world like a young David Bowie. Indeed, some sources claim that the young man is in fact David Bowie. Alas, they're wrong. The photo was taken in 1959, at which time David Bowie (or, to use his real name, David Jones) was 12 years of age.

Bob Marley did, however, work at a car factory – he drove a forklift at a Chrysler factory at Newark, Delaware for a short time in the mid 1960s. He didn't use his real name, however, choosing to use the moniker 'Donald Marley' instead. Marley worked the night shift at the factory, as recounted in the lyrics to his 1976 song '*Night Shift*'.

Q10. *Which F1 team did British Leyland sponsor?*

D.   Williams

Having had comfortably the fastest car during the second half of the 1979 Formula One season, Williams looked well set to continue their run of success in 1980.

Perhaps British Leyland thought so, for they sponsored the team (though not as the title sponsor) for the 1980 and 1981 seasons.

It was an astute choice: Williams won the Constructors' Championship in both 1980 and 1981, and took the Drivers' World Championship in 1980 with driver Alan Jones.

Q1. *All four members of the Beatles owned a Mini Cooper customised by which company?*

C. Radford

In 1966, the Beatles' manager, Brian Epstein, gave a special present to each of the four Beatles: a Mini specially customised by noted coachbuilder Harold Radford.

Each of the four cars was unique. Paul McCartney's Mini was a Cooper S in California Sage Green, an Aston Martin colour, with leather seats, a full-length fabric sunroof, halogen lights, and fog lights built into the grille.

Ringo Starr's Mini was finished in a two-tone colour scheme, with its roof, pillars, door tops and scuttle being finished in silver-grey, and the rest of the bodywork being in Rolls Royce Regal Red. Ringo wanted to be able to fit a drum kit into his Mini, so it featured a hatchback rear and folding rear seat, an option offered by Radford.

John Lennon's Mini bore more relation to The Rolling Stones than the Beatles, in that whomever came up with its colour scheme decided to, well, paint it black. And not just the car - the wheels and seats were also black, and the side and rear windows were tinted a very dark hue.

Of the four cars, it was that of George Harrison that came to be the most memorable. It was initially black in colour and its specification included a full-length sunroof and the rear lights of a VW Beetle. It didn't stay that way for long, however, as it soon received a custom paint job by Dutch artists Simon Posthuma and Marijke Koger to reflect George's new-found interest in Indian culture. It appeared in that guise in the Beatles' Magical Mystery Tour film. It was later given by Harrison to his good friend Eric Clapton, who decided to dispense with Harrison's custom paint scheme. Clapton hung onto the Mini for a while before eventually returning it to Harrison.

All four Minis still exist. Two of them – those originally belonging to Paul McCartney and Ringo Starr – have sold at auction in the last few years. McCartney's Mini, which has long-since been kept in the USA, fetched a remarkable £182,000 in 2018, and that of Starr fetched £102,000 in 2017 – it's now owned by former Spice Girl, Geri Horner.

Of the other two, George Harrison's car is owned by his widow, Olivia. But whilst John Lennon's Mini is believed to remain in the UK, details of its whereabouts and current condition are not in the public domain.

Q2. *Who crashed his McLaren F1 road car, reportedly resulting in an insurance payout of over £900,000?*

D. Rowan Atkinson

Comedian and actor Rowan Atkinson is very much a petrolhead. Cars he either owns or has owned include a 1939 BMW 328, several Aston Martins, and a McLaren F1. Futhermore, he's not only appeared as a racing driver on screen (he played Bentley Boy and double Le Mans winner '*Tim*' *Birkin* in the excellent 1995 TV film *Full Throttle*) but has raced himself, both in modern cars and in historics.

He driving record is not, however, without incident. Like most racers, he's had a few bumps and off-track excursions while racing, but his most significant – and expensive – accident took place on the A605 near to Peterborough in 2011. Atkinson was at the wheel of his McLaren F1 when it left the road and struck a tree, resulting in the actor sustaining relatively minor injuries. The car was, however, extensively damaged.

The car was repaired at considerable expense – it is said that Atkinson's insurers paid out over £900,000 - and was returned to the road. It was Atkinson's second crash in the car, having hit the rear of a Rover Metro in 1999.

Atkinson no longer owns the McLaren. Having purchased it in 1999 for just over £500,000, he sold it in 2015 for a reported £8,000,000.

Q3. *Which former Jaguar chairman held Ministerial office as H.M. Paymaster General?*

A. **Geoffrey Robinson**

Geoffrey Robinson served as an MP from 1976 to 2019. He briefly rose to Ministerial rank, serving as H.M. Paymaster General from May 1997 until December 1998.

Prior to becoming an MP, Robinson had worked for the Industrial Reorganisation Corporation in the late 1960s. He joined British Leyland in 1970 and, though not an accountant, became its Financial Controller a few months later. In 1972, he became the Chairman of Innocenti, BL's Italian subsidiary, and the following year he became Chairman of Jaguar, then also owned by BL.

Robinson's departure from BL in 1975 did not mark the end of his involvement in the motor industry, as he was subsequently involved with Triumph Motorcycles (Meriden) Limited as a non-executive director.

Q4. *Tony Crook was the somewhat distinctive owner of which British car manufacturer?*

A. **Bristol**

Born in 1920, Tony Crook was a successful racing driver in the post-war era, although he only competed in two Grands Prix: the 1952 and 1953 British Grands Prix, each time as a private entrant.

In 1960, Crook became part-owner (and sole distributor) of Bristol Cars Limited, it having been deemed surplus to requirements following the absorption of its erstwhile owner, Bristol Aeroplane Company, into the newly-formed British Aircraft Corporation.

Bristol Cars was – and remained – a small company. Its sole manufacturing facility was located in Bristol, and its only showroom (and, later, headquarters) was situated on Kensington High Street. Crook became the sole owner of the company in 1973 and remained so until he sold 50% of it in 1997.

Like the cars his company made, Tony Crook was idiosyncratic. He was also smart, witty and, above all, passionate about Bristol cars. Stories about him abound. He seldom published production or sales figures, declined to loan cars to motoring journalists and, on one occasion, promptly closed the showroom when he saw film director Michael Winner heading towards it.

It's said that at one British Motor Show he dressed up as a rich Middle East potentate and 'ordered' a number of cars from rival manufacturers. On another occasion, a man whom Crook had paid to dress (and smell) like a tramp took up residence on the stand occupied by one of Bristol's competitors!

Tony Crook died in 2014. We shan't see his like again.

Q5. *John Glenn was ribbed by his fellow Mercury astronauts for owning which car?*

C. NSU Prinz

When John Glenn joined NASA's Project Mercury in 1959, he had built up an enviable reputation as a pilot, having flown fighter aircraft in both the Second World War and the Korean War and been awarded the Distinguished Flying Cross on six occasions. He had also served as a test pilot for the US Navy and set a new speed record for flying across the USA from one coast to the other.

Given that speed had been and - as an astronaut - would continue to be a large factor in Glenn's life, it would be reasonable to assume that he, like most of his fellow astronauts, was a fan of sports cars and fast driving. However, much to the surprise of his peers, Glenn eschewed sports cars in favour of one of the slowest cars it was possible to buy new in the USA – an NSU Prinz. Glenn's reasoning for choosing the Prinz was that he had to use it to travel a long distance to visit his family and he was keen to save money to provide for his children's education rather than spend it on petrol.

Even so, Glenn's choice of car was the subject of some good-natured ribbing at the hands of his fellow astronauts. However, it was he who had the final word on the matter when he scrawled a quotation lifted from *Reader's Digest* on a board in the astronauts' meeting room: "Definition of a sports car: a hedge against the male menopause."

Q6. *Great Train Robber Bruce Reynolds bought which car (in cash) on the day after the robbery?*

B. Austin-Healey 3000

Thought to be the mastermind behind the Great Train Robbery, when £2.6 million was stolen from the Glasgow to London mail train on 8th August 1963, Bruce Reynolds was also a lover of fast cars.

Consequently, he wasted little time in heading to The Chequered Flag, a garage in Chiswick which was renowned for specialising in sports cars, and purchasing a black Austin-Healey 3000 Mark II using cash from the robbery. Needless to say, he gave a false address for the purchase receipt.

Reynolds spent the next five years on the run, eventually being apprehended in 1968. He was sentenced to 25 years in jail for his part in the crime but was released in 1978.

As for the car itself, it was impounded by police and sold off at the Great Train Robbery Special Auction Sale in 1969. It was sold again at auction in 2004, at which time it fetched £27,000. It still exists and is currently on SORN.

Q7. *The orange globes at UK pedestrian crossings were informally named after whom?*

B. Leslie Hore-Belisha

Leslie Hore-Belisha served for 22 years as a Member of Parliament and held Ministerial office from 1932 to 1940.

Although history records that he was Secretary of State for War when the Second World War broke out, his most significant Ministerial appointment was that of Transport Minister, a post he occupied from 1934 to 1937.

The Road Traffic Act 1930 had abolished all speed limits and this, coupled with increasing numbers of cars on the road, resulted in an increase in deaths and injuries attributable to road accidents. In 1934, 7343 people died in road accidents in the UK with a further 231,603 being injured. Hore-Belisha was fortunate not to become one of them, narrowly avoiding being struck by a speeding sports car in Camden High Street soon after taking up his post at the Ministry of Transport.

Clearly, action was required, and Hore-Belisha took it. It was he who introduced the Road Traffic Act 1934 which, to the dismay of some, imposed a new 30 mph speed limit in urban areas, as well as introducing compulsory driving tests in the UK. In addition, he also introduced a new, much more comprehensive version of the Highway Code.

Impressive though that is, he is best remembered for a simple but effective road safety measure – adding orange globes to the poles that mark pedestrian crossings. These globes quickly became known by the public as 'Belisha beacons', and the name has stuck to this day.

Q8. *Major Ivan Hirst is credited with saving which car manufacturer?*

C. Volkswagen

In the immediate aftermath of World War 2, Ivan Hirst, a Major in the Royal Electrical & Mechanical Engineers, arrived in the German town of Wolfsburg to take charge of what remained of its vehicle factory.

The factory itself was heavily damaged but Hirst found that the plant's power generating station could be made to work and, to his surprise, also discovered that much of the machinery was intact, having been dispersed into the countryside. He therefore decided to put the plant to work producing vehicles for the British military.

After his original plan to produce Kübelwagens had to be abandoned due to a lack of body panels, he found that it was possible to make Beetles instead. The British Army ordered 20,000 of them, and Hirst and the plant were in business. Makeshift repairs were carried out to the factory with whatever was available – which was very little at first – and production commenced.

By March 1946, the factory was producing 1000 cars a month, and by the following year, it was able to start exporting vehicles. It continued to grow: by May 1948, it employed 8,700 people, and the year after that it formally returned to German control.

Q9. *Which car formerly owned by Princess Diana sold at auction for £52,640 in 2021?*

B. Ford Escort Ghia

The Austin Metro was the first car to be associated with Princess Diana, it having been her mode of transport when she, then known as Lady Diana Spencer, was first romantically linked with Prince Charles. The Metro was sold in June 1981 and is now on display in the Coventry Transport Museum.

It was replaced by a 1.6 litre Ford Escort Ghia that was given to her by Prince Charles as an engagement gift. She was regularly pictured in the car both prior to her marriage and in the early months of it. The Escort was sold in 1982 following the birth of Prince William.

It resurfaced periodically, most recently in June 2021, when it was sold at auction to a museum in Chile for a staggering £52,640, several times the price that a standard Escort 1.6 litre Ghia would fetch.

Princess Diana owned other Escorts in the 1980s, including a series 1 RS Turbo Custom. This car, built in 1985, differed from standard RS Turbos in several ways: it had a different grille from that fitted to RS models; it was fitted with a second interior mirror (for use by the Princess's bodyguard); and it was painted in a colour – black - in which RS Turbo Customs were not normally available. That said, it wasn't the only black RS Turbo: two identical cars were ordered for use as decoys.

Diana's RS Turbo Custom is presently owned by a collector. Should he ever decide to sell it, the chances are that it will make comfortably more than the £60,168 paid for an RS Custom at auction in 2015.

Q10. *Director John Boorman once took to the Pacific Coast Highway with whom on the roof of the car he was driving?*

C.   **Lee Marvin**

One evening in the late 1960s, film director John Boorman and his good friend, actor Lee Marvin, had dinner together at a restaurant in Santa Monica, California.

Nothing unusual about that, you might think. Except that Marvin got so drunk that a concerned Boorman took the actor's car keys from him and got into the driving seat of Marvin's car. But if he expected Marvin to join him in the car, he was mistaken, for Marvin instead climbed onto its roof and refused to get off it.

Unable to persuade Marvin to budge and unwilling to wait all night for him to do so, Boorman tentatively set off down the Pacific Coast Highway towards Marvin's home in Malibu. He hadn't travelled very far when he was stopped by a policeman on a motorcyle. When Boorman pulled over, the traffic cop's first words to him were: "Sir, do you know that you have Lee Marvin on the roof of your car?"

In the end, no harm was done. Marvin got home safely, he and Boorman remained friends, and the traffic cop got to dine out on a story so bizarre that few, if any, Hollywood scriptwriters could have dreamed it up.

PROTOYPES AND CONCEPTS 9

Q1. *The Equus was a 1978 prototype built by which company?*

D. Vauxhall

A product of Vauxhall's Luton Styling Studio and Wayne Cherry, its Design Director, the Equus concept car was a silver two-seat convertible that emphasised sharp angles over curves, had fared-in headlamps and a rather obvious rake from rear to front.

The sole Equus prototype was not built by Vauxhall but Panther Westwinds, a small British manufacturer with a reputation for the build quality of their cars, one of which – the retro-styled Lima sports car - used a Vauxhall chassis and engine.

Its probably fair to say that Panther was eyeing the possibility of being afforded a bigger role in the Equus project should Vauxhall decide to put it into production. Had that happened, it might well have saved Panther from going bust in 1980. But at a time when sports car sales were starting to flag, Vauxhall decided that the Equus would never progress beyond an interesting styling exercise. A pity, for there's little doubt that, with the running gear available to Vauxhall, it could quite easily have been made to go as good as it looked.

File under 'lost opportunities'.

Q2. *In what year did a company then co-owned by British Leyland produce a prototype electric car based on a Mini platform?*

C. 1972

One of the less well-known parts of the British Leyland conglomeration was a small company that produced electrically-powered vehicles, then known as Crompton Leyland Electricars Limited.

In 1971, Michelotti was commissioned to produce a design for a prototype electric car based on the Mini platform. The resulting car, the profile of which looked not unlike a compressed AMC Gremlin, had a GRP bodyshell and was powered by 24 lead-acid batteries. Its top speed was a little over 30 miles per hour and it had a maximum range of around 40 miles.

With some development, it might have made an ideal city car, but it was destined to remain a one-off. BL sold its 50% share in Crompton Leyland Electricars in 1972 and turned away from electrically-powered vehicles.

The prototype still exists, however, and can be seen at the British Motor Museum at Gaydon.

Q3. *The Talbot Wind was a one-off prototype created by which coachbuilder?*

C. Heuliez

Given that it was a leisure vehicle based, like the Matra-Simca Rancho, on the Simca 1100 van, it's perhaps understandable that some people assume that the Talbot Wind was simply another version of the Rancho. But that wasn't the case.

Instead, the Wind was made by Heuliez, a French automotive design studio, coachbuilder and vehicle manufacturer. And although it dates from 1980, its maker had been working with Simca 1100s since 1968, several years before Matra started work on what would become the Rancho.

It's probably true to say that the Wind was inspired by the success of the Rancho, but it's equally true to say that it also owes something to Heuliez's original Simca 1100 prototype of 1968, the Saharienne. Like the Wind, the Saharienne was also a pick-up aimed at recreational rather than business users, although unlike the Wind it was also a convertible.

Finished in white with white alloy wheels, blue stripes, large 'Wind decals', surfboard racks, and roof-mounted spotlights, the Wind prototype certainly looked the part. It might have sold reasonably well had it been offered in places with a warm climate and inviting beaches, but it remained a one-off.

The prototype Wind is believed to still exist. It formed part of Heuliez's collection for many years but was auctioned off in 2012 along with 39 other Heuliez prototypes.

Q4. What was the model designation of Porsche's 1980s small roadster project?

B. 984

In the 1980s, Porsche came close to augmenting its range by introducing a small, light and (by Porsche standards) inexpensive roadster, the 984.

Powered by a rear-mounted 2.0 litre four-cylinder 'boxer' engine, the 984 range was to include a version with what was then an innovative folding hardtop roof. There was even talk at one time of the 984 having four-wheel drive but it's unlikely that it would have featured on production cars, at least initially.

Running prototypes were built and tested, and the project was at a fairly advanced stage when it was canned in late 1987, a victim of the fall-out from that October's Stock Market crash which wreaked havoc on the world's stock markets and sparked fears of a major global recession.

Q5. *The original Panther Solo was to have been powered by which engine?*

B. Ford 1.6 litre CVH

In its original guise, Panther had largely concentrated on building cars that mixed modern mechanicals with retro style.

Following the financial collapse of Panther in 1980, its assets were purchased by a South Korean company and Young Chul Kim was installed as Managing Director. But although the new Panther company resumed production of cars using the modern/retro recipe, Kim had his eye on producing a sports car that was contemporary in every respect.

The new car, styled by Ken Greenley and with a chassis by Len Bailey, was to be a mid-engined sports car powered the fuel-injected version of Ford's 1.6 litre CVH engine, and it was to be ready for production by 1986.

Kim had hoped to build 1500 to 2000 examples of the new car – the Panther Solo – a year, but his plans were changed by the arrival of the Toyota MR2. Unable to compete with the MR2's proposed US price tag of under $9000, Kim halted the Solo project in its original guise.

The Solo was duly reinvented as a more upmarket sports car, and eventually went on sale as the more advanced, more powerful and considerably more expensive Solo 2. But that is, as they say, another story.

Q6. *Which design house was responsible for the 1972 Citroën GS Camargue prototype?*

C. Bertone

Remember the commercial for the Citroën BX GTI 16V, the one that featured Marcello Gandini? Well, this is where his (and Bertone's) association with Citroën began.

When it was launched in 1970, the GS was nothing short of remarkable. Packed with technology, it offered big-car comfort in a small package. And it looked great too.

But even the svelte, modern lines of the GS were eclipsed by those of the Camargue, Bertone's low, glassy, and aerodynamic take on a GS coupé. Indeed, it looked like an ultra-modern, continent-shrinking GT car. Until, that is, you either started it or took a peek under its bonnet – a clamshell hinged at the A pillars – and were confronted by its 1015cc flat-four engine.

That said, the Camargue's combination of arresting looks and fuel-efficient engine would have made it a very stylish way in which to affordably navigate the energy crisis that hit hard in the aftermath of the 1973 Yom Kippur War. Alas, with Citroën's finances in something of a mess, it was destined to be a one-off.

Q7. *The Triplex 10-20 was a one-off shooting brake conversion of which car?*

D. Princess

If you're ever wondered what you'd get if you were to take a car that should have been a hatchback but wasn't, add in a design house with an excellent track record, and mix it with a glazing company looking for a rolling promotional vehicle, then wonder no longer – the Triplex 10-20 is that car.

It's a matter of record – not to say bewilderment - that BL made a conscious decision not to endow the Princess with a hatchback. Instead, it was left to others, such as Crayford, to convert standard cars into more practical hatchback models. But good as those aftermarket con versions were, it was Ogle Design who really showed the motoring world what the Princess could and should have been.

Conceived at the behest of Triplex, who wanted to showcase their automotive glass technology, Carl Olsen of Ogle Design took a standard Princess, removed the chrome detailing, gave it polycarbonate bumpers, added a new front grille, and transformed the rear of the car by turning it from a booted fastback into a glassy shooting brake. An ultra-thin sunroof and decals that, to modern eyes, look like they've been appropriated from the 1980s completed what was – and is – a very appealing makeover.

Only one 10-20 was made. It made its debut at the 1978 British Motor Show and was thereafter used for a time as a promotional vehicle. It's still around today and can be found at the British Motor Museum at Gaydon.

Q8. *Which Ford concept car evolved into the Sierra?*

A. Probe III

Let's start by clearing something up: yes, the Coins, Megastar II and 021c really were all Ford prototypes!

But for present purposes, it's the Probe III that's of interest to us. So named because it was the third a series of a concept cars, the Probe III was first shown at the 1981 Frankfurt Motor Show.

Its purpose was to prepare the public for the Sierra, the 'jellymould' looks of which were far removed from both the Cortina that it would replace and the cars it must compete against for market share. Quite simply, the Probe III would not have existed had Ford not been so concerned about how the public would react to the Sierra's styling.

The same reasoning was behind Ford's decision to make the Probe III a little more radical looking than the Sierra. Consequently, it featured elements, such as fared-in rear wheels, that Ford had no intention of incorporating in production Sierras.

The Probe III's efforts notwithstanding, it took the public a little while to get used to the styling of the Sierra. Indeed, it's tempting to wonder just how well it would have sold had the Probe III not first softened-up the buying public a little.

Q9. *The Fiat X1/23 was a prototype...?*

C. **Electric city car**

First shown in 1972, the lozenge-shaped, two-seat Fiat X1/23 was small, being just 2.66 meters long, and looked rather like a slightly upscaled children's car, due to both its diminutive proportions and its unusual styling.

When it reappeared in 1976, it was fitted with a front-mounted motor that produced just under 19 bhp and drove the front wheels. In spite of having regenerative braking, the X1/23 was burdened by the low power output of its motor and the weight of its rear-mounted batteries and could do no more than 45 miles per hour. Its range of around 50 miles was also somewhat meagre.

Like many electric cars of its era, the X1/23 was destined to become a museum piece rather than give rise to a roadgoing variant. But with vehicles such as the Renault Twizy and the Citroen Ami having now reached the market, perhaps Fiat and the manufacturers of other early EVs missed an opportunity.

Q10. *The Aston Martin DBS V8-based Sotheby Special was designed by…?*

D.   Tom Karen

Commissioned by a tobacco company as a promotional vehicle and styled by Tom Karen of Ogle Design, the Aston Martin DBS V8-based Sotheby Special was first shown at the Montreal International Auto Show in 1972.

The Montreal show car was never registered for the road, but a second, roadworthy, car was commissioned. It shared the show car's colour scheme of dark blue with gold pinstriping, but this was later changed to white with red triangles.

Unlike its parent car, the wedge-shaped Sotheby Special featured bodywork that was fashioned from glassfibre, with its upper surfaces – i.e. those above its waistline – being formed from perspex supported by alloy tubing. At the rear, a single stainless steel panel was home to 22 lights – the idea being that the harder the driver braked, the more lights were illuminated.

Other differences from a standard DBS V8 included lights that were covered by drop-down panels, and a sideways rear seat that accommodated one passenger, thus making it a three-seater.

Both cars – and a third car that was later commissioned by a private individual – still exist. The original Montreal show car, which had been partially stripped and was in 'barn find' condition, sold at auction for £87,750 in 2015.

10

GENERAL KNOWLEDGE 4

Q1. ***Which prototype cars was crashed by its test driver during filming in 1971?***

B. Jaguar XJ13

The XJ13 was a low, swoopy and open prototype that was built in 1966 with a view to racing in the Le Mans 24 Hours but never took part in a single race.

Work on the V12-powered prototype began in 1965 and was completed in March 1966. But rather than test their new car, Jaguar management decreed that it should not be run. However, testing did commence in 1967, by which time Jaguar was now part of British Motor Holdings.

For a time it seemed that the XJ13, suitably developed, might yet get to compete at Le Mans. However, its chances were scuppered when a rule change decreed that the maximum engine capacity of prototypes like the XJ13 would be restricted to 3.0 litres with effect from the 1968 running of the race. The XJ13's engine therefore once more fell silent, and the XJ13 sat mutely under a dust cover.

Three years later, Jaguar was preparing to unveil the V12 version of the E-Type sports car at the Geneva Motor Show. To support this launch, they hit upon the idea of also showing the XJ13, albeit there were a number of differences between its V12 engine and the production version in the E-Type. To that end the XJ13 was taken to the MIRA test track at Nuneaton for a filming session.

With test driver Norman Dewis at the helm, the XJ13 was on its third fast lap, having previously circulated at modest pace, when the right-hand rear wheel gave way. This caused it to slew into a guardrail and spin into the infield, somersaulting several times. Miraculously, Dewis emerged from the wreckage with only minor injuries, and although the car itself was heavily damaged it was subsequently restored, albeit with a few minor modifications.

Today, the XJ13 is on display at the British Motor Museum in Gaydon. Maintained in running condition, it can be seen (and heard) at events in the UK and elsewhere.

Q2. *Which somewhat dilapidated car does Withnail drive in the 1987 film Withnail & I?*

B. Jaguar Mark 2

There's a sense of musty, faded grandeur about *Withnail*, a drunk, failing actor whose first name is never revealed to the viewer. It's therefore entirely appropriate that he should drive a car that's a similar blend of class and creeping ruin: a rusty, smoky and generally decrepit 1961 Jaguar Mark 2.

Rather than reveal the film's plot (it's the sort of film you need to see to appreciate), I'll simply say that fans of classic cars will enjoy spotting the (mostly correct for its 1969 setting) cars that appear in it.

Q3. *Which of the following cars did NOT feature at least one version powered by the Rover K-Series engine?*

C. Rover 600

Having first appeared in 1988, the all-aluminium Rover K-Series engine went on to be produced until the collapse of MG Rover in 2005.

Offered in a range of cubic capacities from 1.1 litre to 1,8 litre, the

K-Series not only powered a bevy of Rovers (including the Metro, 25, 200 and 400) but was also found in the series 1 Lotus Elise, the first-generation Land Rover Freelander, the Caterham 7 and 21, and a number of MG cars. It was not, however, used in the Rover 600.

Of the K-Series' many incarnations, it was its installation in the MGF (and TF) that was most problematic. The essential problem was that the engine was designed for use in a front-engined car, and fitting it to a mid-engined car with a front-mounted radiator gave rise to a number of issues which could result in overheating and a blown head gasket. Indeed, the frequency with which the latter occurred* resulted in wags in the motor trade referring to the MGF as the 'HGF', an acronym for head gasket failure.

* Fixes have long since been found for the main issues, though prospective buyers of an MGF or TF should make sure that they've been implemented in the car they're thinking of buying.

Q4. *The Alfa Romeo Montreal prototypes shown at the 1967 World's Fair were fitted with which engine?*

A.   1570cc 4-cylinder

In its original form, the Alfa Romeo Montreal was the product of a request made to Alfa Romeo to produce a car to be exhibited the '*Man, the producer*' pavilion of the 1967 World's Fair (otherwise known as Expo 67) at Montreal. There was, however, a snag: they only had nine months in which to design and build a car to display.

The resulting car was a clever mixture of existing components – the 1570cc engine from the Giulia 1600 TI, the chassis from the Giulia Sprint GT, and a coupé bodyshell (from Bertone's Marcello Gandini) whose lines swooped and curved in all the right places.

Two examples of the front-engined, 2+2 coupe were shown at Expo 67, causing such a stir that Alfa Romeo decided to put it into production.

It took three years, however, for the production version to appear. Its styling differed very little from that of the prototype, but it now sported a rather more potent engine: a 2.6 litre V8 unit that had been developed from the 2.0 litre engine that powered the Tipo 33 sports-prototype racer. And it now also had a name: Montreal.

In spite of its name, the Montreal was never sold in North America. It was, however, offered in right-hand drive form. In all, 3925 Montreals were built from 1970 to 1977. That said, the thirst of its V8 engine caused sales to fall off sharply as a result of the global energy crisis of the mid-1970s. Indeed, more than 75% of the Montreals produced were built before 1974.

Q5. ***Which of these Volkswagen saloons was the first to go on sale?***

C. Derby

There was a time when new Volkswagens (well, at least the European market versions) were either partly or wholly related to winds.

That changed in 1977 with the arrival of the Derby, the booted version of the Polo (if you're wondering, the Polo's name refers to polar winds as well as to the sport). In the UK, the Derby was sold until the demise of the mark 1 Polo in 1981.

The Jetta, named after the jet stream, was introduced in 1979 as the name for the booted version of the VW Golf. The name was used for the first two generations of Golf saloons in Europe, but it was dropped in favour of the name Vento (there's that wind thing again...) for the third generation.

The Vento name was used for only one generation of the booted Golf (1993-1999), with fourth-generation models bearing the name Bora (it's – you guessed it – a wind) instead. In 2005, however, Volkswagen dusted off the Jetta name for the fifth-generation Golf saloon, although the Bora name continued to be used in certain markets. Confusing, eh?

That leaves us with Santana. No, not the famous guitarist but the booted version of the Passat. The Santana name was first used in 1983 in certain markets, and briefly in Europe from 1984. Oh, and if you're wondering its name refers to the Santa Ana winds.

Q6. *Louis Malle's 1973 documentary film 'Humain, trop humain' focused on which car manufacturer?*

D.   **Citroën**

Okay, I'll admit it – I didn't know much about Louis Malle before writing this book. So for those who, like I was, are a little bit in the dark about Monsieur Malle, here's some brief information about him.

Born in 1932, Malle jointly won (with co-director Jacques Cousteau) the Palme D'Or at Cannes in 1956 and the Academy Award for Best Documentary in 1957 for *Le Monde du silence*, a film which made innovative use of underwater cameras to show the undersea world in colour.

Malle thereafter made a number of films about controversial and taboo subjects as well as more mainstream films, such as the 1980 Hollywood crime drama, *Atlantic City*.

In 1973, Malle directed *Humain, trop humain*, a documentary film about the Citroën factory in Rennes, with a sequence shot at the annual Paris Salon de L'Auto. Though not a silent film, it has no voiceover track nor are there any interviews. As such, it offers an unvarnished record of a particular time as well as some interesting visual insights into how cars were once made.

It's well worth tracking down, although the DVD version is not available at the time of writing.

Q7. *In 1965, which car set a record by achieving sales of over 1,000,000 examples in the USA in a single year?*

B. Chevrolet Impala

Introduced in 1958 as a range-topping version of the Chevrolet Bel Air, the Impala soon became a discrete model in its own right. Indeed, such was the dizzying pace at which Detroit refreshed its model ranges that 1965 saw the Impala reach its fourth generation.

By modern standards, the Impala was a large car (almost 17 and a half feet long) and was powered by a range of engines that ranged from a 3.8 litre six-cylinder unit to a 6.7 litre V8 (although this was discontinued in favour of 6.5 litre unit early in the 1965 production run). With fuel prices low in the USA, the Impala had become well established as a popular family car by the time the 1965 model came around.

For 1965, Chevrolet had sought to enhance the model's appeal by giving it cleaner and more modern lines than its predecessors. There were also suspension improvements but the emphasis was very much on evolution rather than revolution. It was an approach that worked, with 1,074,925 Impalas being sold in the USA in 1965. It was – and remains – the highest annual sales volume ever recorded* in the USA by a single car. And just for good measure, the Impala also broke the million sales mark again in 1966.

*It's possible that the Ford Model T may have sold more examples in a single year but in the absence of records to verify this, the Impala reigns supreme in that respect.

Q8. *In which country was height-adjustable suspension banned from 1974 to 1981?*

D. USA

Ever wondered why the Citroën SM disappeared prematurely from the US market?

The answer has its origins in the National Traffic and Motor Vehicle Safety Act 1966, which authorized the federal government to set and regulate standards for motor vehicles and highways, a necessary step given in circumstances which, as President Johnson mentioned when signing the Act, saw 614 Americans die in automobile accidents over the Labor (sic) Day weekend in 1966.

As a result of the Act, the National Highway Traffic Safety Administration issued numerous mandatory Standards, including Standard 215 on Exterior Protection. Under this Standard, the height at which bumpers (fenders in the USA) sat above the ground would be standardised.

As the height of the SM's bumpers varied according to the height to which its adjustable hydropneumatic suspension had been set, Citroen had little choice but to withdraw the SM from the US market.

Standard 215 also covered the ability of bumpers to resist low-speed impacts without causing damage to the vehicle's lights, fuel tank and pipes, exhaust and cooling systems, and door, boot and bonnet latches. So if you've ever wondered why BL fitted rubber bumpers to the MGB and raised its ride height by an inch, you need wonder no more...

Q9. Which Porsche was reintroduced to the range six years after its deletion?

B. 912

Introduced in 1965 as an entry-level version of the 911, the Porsche 912 was originally equipped with a 1.6 flat-four engine that delivered 89 bhp. And although it was slower than the bigger-engined 911, the 912 was lighter, nimbler and more fuel-efficient. The 912 sold well and even outsold the 911 for a time. However, the arrival of the cheaper, 110 bhp 911T in 1967 affected sales of the 912. Even so, more than 32,000 were built between 1965 and 1969, when it made way for the new 914.

The 912's days weren't quite at an end, though, as it made a brief return in 1975. Dubbed the 912E, this version was powered by the same 2.0 litre flat-four VW Type 4 engine as had powered some late-model 914s. Produced as a stop-gap model pending the arrival of the 924, the 912E was sold only in the USA.

Production of the 912E ended in 1976 after 2,092 had been built.

Q10. *In what year did TVR's factory at Blackpool close?*

B.   **2006**

Founded in 1949 by Blackpool-born Trevor Wilkinson, the marque was based in Blackpool for close to six decades in spite of changes in both ownership and fortune, which included both receivership and liquidation.

TVR's survival into a new millennium owed everything to Peter Wheeler, a chemical engineer who had rescued the company from near-certain doom in 1981 and thereafter kept it going in the face of a never-ending string of legislative and financial challenges.

After nearly a quarter of a century at TVR's helm, Wheeler sold his shareholding to Nikolai Smolenski, the son of a Russian tycoon. Wheeler, however, retained ownership of the land on which the TVR factory stood.

Smolenski's stated aim was to keep TVR in Blackpool but in 2006, having laid off much of the workforce a few months earlier in the face of falling sales, Smolenski announced that TVR production would move to Turin. That never happened but TVR production nonetheless ceased and the Blackpool factory lay dormant.

Much has happened over the years since then, with the most significant development being the rise of a new company, TVR Automotive Limited. As as the time of writing, no new production TVR has yet emerged but the company hopes to release an all-new incarnation of the TVR Griffith in 2022.

11

LESSER SPOTTED CLASSICS

Q1. *The Panther Rio was based on which car?*

A. Triumph Dolomite

In its 1970s guise, the marque is best known for producing cars that were a fusion of retro style and modern running gear. Its output included the riotously expensive De Ville, a handbuilt car with the looks of a 1930s Bugatti, the running gear of a contemporary Jaguar and an epic price tag.

The fuel crisis of the mid-1970s resulted in the demand for expensive, gas-guzzling cars slackening for a time. But where others saw woe, Panther owner Robert Jankel saw an opportunity. He believed that a car which was both opulent and fuel efficient would undoubtedly appeal to the wealthy customer who wanted luxury, superior build quality and good fuel consumption in one package.

The result was the Panther Rio, essentially a restyled, luxuriously trimmed Triumph Dolomite. Launched in 1975, Panther claimed – not without some justification – that it was finished to Rolls Royce standards. Two versions were available: the standard car with a Triumph 1850cc engine, and the Especial, which used the 2.0 litre 16 valve unit from the Dolomite Sprint. Neither was cheap, however, and it was price that proved to be the Rio's achilles heel – the Especial cost considerably more than a 5.3 litre Jaguar XJ, and nearly three times as much as a Dolomite Sprint.

Had the fuel crisis continued to bite, perhaps the Rio might have found more buyers, but as it was only 38 were built in the two years in which it was produced.

Q2. *The Fiesta Fly convertible was originally produced by which company?*

B.   Crayford

Crayford Engineering was well known for producing estate and convertible versions of production cars that lacked such models in their range. Indeed, over the years Crayford's products included convertible versions of the Mini, the Austin 1100 and various Fords, including the Capri.

In 1981 Crayford produced a convertible version of the Ford Fiesta, which they dubbed the Fiesta Fly. With no roll-over hoops and a soft top that folded flat, the Fly had a flat rear deck. But this came at a price: the Fly's bootlid was welded shut and access to its cargo space was only possible from within the car. That said, the conversion was a good one; the Fly even passed the acid test of looking good with its hood up.

After around 30 cars were built, Crayford struck a deal with F. English Engineering of Bournemouth whereby the latter took over the project.

As a conversion of an existing car, the Fly was available in the same engine and trim guises as the standard Fiesta, including the XR2. It was, however, rather more expensive than the standard car, which limited sales.

The cars sold by Crayford and F. English were based on the mark 1 Fiesta, with over 200 being built. English did produce a handful of mark 2 versions but then sold the project to a Dutch company, AGM Kinesis.

AGM retained the Fly name for a short time but this was dropped when they launched a revised version, with an opening boot, a different hood design and a new name – the Fiesta Flirt.

Q3. *What Rover Group car was offered as a 'BRM' limited edition?*

D. Rover 200

There's a school of thought that says that every car needs a halo model in its range, to boost its image and help increase showroom traffic.

In the early 1990s, however, Rover lacked such a model. For all that the company produced some good cars, its image could be said to be of a marque for people who wore tweed and twinsets rather than as a purveyor of cars for driving enthusiasts.

Producing a coupé version of the Rover 200 was one solution, the resulting car being handsome and, particularly in the case of the somewhat wayward 220 Turbo built between 1992 and 1995, rapid.

The other solution was to produce a limited edition version of the Rover 200 Vi, one that harked back to Rover's collaboration with BRM on the gas turbine-powered racing car which contested the Le Mans 24 Hours in 1963 and 1965.

Having tested the water with a proof of concept version at several international motor shows in 1997, Rover decided to put the Rover 200 BRM into production. Launched at the British Motor Show in 1998, the 200 BRM owed only its name (used under permission) and orange air intake to the famous Bourne marque.

The 200 BRM was powered by the same 143 bhp unit fitted to standard 200 Vi models, but it sat on lowered and stiffened suspension, had a close-ratio gearbox and delivered its power via a Torque-sensing differential. Inside, it was distinguished from lesser 200s by having red quilted leather seats and door panels, red carpeting, a two-tone (red and black) steering wheel, and aluminium heater controls and trim.

It went fairly well, had good handling and...was too expensive. Introduced very late in the Rover 200's model life, it struggled to attract buyers at its initial £18,000 price point. This led Rover to drop the price, first to £16,000 and later to £13,495 (a special price for the month of September 1999 only).

All told, 1115 Rover BRMs were built, of which all but 312 were for the UK market. Today, around 90 examples are registered with the DVLA, with another 250 or so being on SORN.

Q4. *Which animal featured on the Gordon-Keeble marque badge?*

A. Tortoise

You might think that from its badge that Gordon-Keeble made cars that were slow and steady, like the tortoise of Aesop's fable. If so, you'd be wrong, for the marque's sole offering was a stylish sports saloon powered by a V8 Chevrolet lump.

The story of how it came to be is too long to rehearse fully here but suffice it to say that the car that became the Gordon-Keeble was based on a suggestion by an American pilot, styled by Giorgetto Giugiaro and built in the UK.

It first appeared on the Bertone stand at the 1960 Geneva Motor Show as the Gordon GT, the Italian company having produced the body shell. Although very much a prototype, it received a warm reception. Indeed, it was road-tested twice by *Autocar* that year, drawing much praise for its performance. It was also taken to Detroit and shown to Chevrolet senior management, who were sufficiently impressed to agree to provide its makers with the same V8 engine as the Corvette. And then things went a little awry.

The car was undeniably attractive but it was only financially viable if it could be produced in sufficiently large numbers to not only pay the bills but generate a profit. For that, major backers were required. None, however, could be found. Undeterred, Gordon-Keeble put it into production anyway.

Unfortunately, cash-flow issues soon arose and Gordon-Keeble Ltd. went into liquidation. The company's assets were, however, bought from the liquidator and a new company, Keeble Cars Limited, was formed. A few more cars were built but production ended in 1967 after a total of 99 cars had been built. One more car was built from spares in 1971.

As for the tortoise? Well, the story seems to be that a pet tortoise sauntered into the middle of an early photo shoot, leading to its adoption as the marque badge.

And in one way, that's appropriate. It's understood that as many as 90 Gordon-Keebles have survived to the present day, albeit not all of them are currently on the road. That compares well with many cars built in significantly larger numbers. In that sense, perhaps Aesop was right.

Q5. *The Indian-made Sipani Dolphin was based on which European car?*

C. **Reliant Kitten**

Launched in 1975, the Reliant Kitten was a small, four-wheel, front-engined car (available in hatchback and, later, estate/van guises) that used the same 848cc engine as Reliant's three-wheel offerings and had a fibreglass body.

Although the Kitten's size and low weight meant that it was both manoeuvrable and economical, it was relatively expensive – a consequence of being built by a low-volume manufacturer unable to benefit from the economies of scale enjoyed by larger companies. Consequently, its sales figures topped out at a few hundred examples each year: total Kitten production from 1975 until its demise in 1982 was 4551.

Sipani, an Indian company, acquired the rights to make the Kitten in India, choosing to give it a new name: Dolphin. When production commenced in 1982, the company bullishly stated that it already had orders for the first two years production run, some 6000 cars. As it transpired, however, fewer than 2000 Dolphins were built between 1982 and the end of production in 1987.

Production of a mark 2 Dolphin – known as the Montana – commenced in 1987. A five-door version was introduced followed by one powered by a 901cc three-cylinder diesel engine. However, although production continued into the 1990s, the Montana – like the Kitten and Dolphin – never sold in appreciable numbers.

Q6. *What was the name given to the styling of the Triumph Mayflower?*

C. Razor Edge

In the aftermath of World War 2, the UK was heavily in debt, its export markets had shrunk, and much of its merchant shipping fleet sat at the bottom of the sea. So bad was the situation that economist John Maynard Keynes stated that the UK faced a financial Dunkirk unless it could obtain a loan of 5 billion US dollars.

It got that money, thanks to the USA and Canada, but even so it was imperative to maximise earnings from exports. In this time of need, the motor industry came to the rescue, with British manufacturers taking full advantage of the fact that demand for new cars in the USA and Australia exceeded the ability of local manufacturers to meet it. Indeed, Britain soon established itself as the leading exporter of cars in the world, a position it would hold for several years.

Little time was wasted in getting new cars into production. Indeed, when the Triumph Mayflower was launched in 1949 it was the third new post-war Triumph. More compact than its siblings, it was intended to cater for what its makers presumably felt was pent-up demand in both the USA and elsewhere for an upmarket small car. As such, comfort rather than performance (63 mph and 0-50 mph in 26.6 seconds) lay at the very top of its creators' list of priorities.

Its styling was hardly forward-looking. Instead, the Mayflower's upright, angular lines were of a type popularly known as 'razor edge' or 'knife edge'. Styling of this sort had hitherto been the province of large luxury cars. By adopting it for the compact Mayflower, the intention was to convey an impression of quality and comfort. And whatever the Mayflower's other faults, it was a comfortable car that was roomy for its size.

It had been hoped that the Mayflower would be a hit with overseas customers, but only 510 examples were sold in the USA. Indeed, its production run of just over 34,000 fell far short of expectations, and the last Mayflower was produced in 1953.

Q7. *The Campero was a Spanish-built utility vehicle based on which car?*

B. Simca 1200

There was a time when it was much easier for small, low-volume enterprises to build cars which went on retail sale. The Campero is one such vehicle.

Based on a Simca 1200 (the Spanish market version of the Simca 1100) chassis, it was designed by Antoni Madueño and was first shown at the 1972 Barcelona Motor Show. It retained the Simca running gear but featured a new body, originally fabricated from metal but later fashioned out of GRP. The result was a vehicle that looked not unlike a more angular version of the Citroën Mehari.

Chrysler's support for the project was rather less than wholehearted. Whilst they agreed to supply Simca 1200 platforms and running gear to the Campero's manufacturers, Autotecnica, they did not include it in Chrysler Spain's model range. Accordingly, Autotecnica had to make their own arrangements for distribution of the Campero.

That hindered sales, as did the Campero's price. It was rather more expensive than a standard Simca 1200 and, more tellingly, quite a bit pricier than a Mehari. Its better performance made up for some of that price differential but buyers were very thin on the ground. Indeed, it's reputed that only 35 were sold in the two years following its launch in 1973.

In 1975, a Barcelona-based Simca dealership, Talleres Panades, took over the Campero project. Under their stewardship, the Campero received a somewhat ungainly restyle, its character changing from an open car with a soft top to a mini-SUV with a hard top. At the same time, the 1118cc engine of the original was replaced by a larger (1294cc) and more powerful engine. In this new guise, the Campero continued to be sold until 1979. It was not, however, a big seller, with only 54 examples being produced.

The Campero's main claim to fame is that it may to some degree have inspired the creation of a much more successful adaptation of the Simca 1100/1200: the Matra Rancho.

Q8. *What was the model designation of the first car produced by Noble Automotive?*

A. M10

Noble Automotive is perhaps best known for the M12, a mid-engined coupé powered by a turbocharged Ford Duratec engine. The M12 sold well and established Noble as a manufacturer of focused, high-performance cars for enthusiastic drivers.

It was not, however, the company's first offering. That car was the M10 of 1999, a two-seat convertible powered by a normally aspirated 2.5 litre version of the Duratec engine.

Although the M10 went and handled well and drew praise for its build quality, it was almost immediately superseded by the M12. The result was a production run of only 6 cars. A pity, for it was capable of giving the Lotus and Porsche opposition something of a run for their money whilst offering an al fresco driving experience if its driver so desired.

Q9. *Torcars of Devon offered a camper van conversion of which car?*

D. Morris Marina

Torcars was a Devon-based company which, for the most part, specialised in converting cars and vans into camper vans (or, if you prefer, motorhomes).

Its roots lay in a Suusex-based concern, R. Webster & Co., which converted vehicles into camper vans to customers' specifications. One such customer was Alan Hutchinson. Impressed with the work done by Webster to his own vehicle, he made enquiries about investing in the company.

The result was a new company, Torcars. A site for a factory near Torrington, Devon, was chosen, with the company meantime operating out of premises in Torrington High Street.

The new factory opened in 1971, producing camper van conversions of several popular cars and vans, including the Morris Marina. Like all camper conversions produced by the company, it was known as a SunTor – or, to give it its full name, the SunTor Marina Motor Caravan.

In 1973, W. Mumford Ltd. acquired a 50% share in Torcars. This opened up a second production facility for Torcars in Plymouth, where Torcars-branded vehicles (notably a convertible version of the Marina and a hatchback version of the Princess) were built in addition to the camper vans produced in Devon.

TorCars ceased trading in 1979 but was subsequently purchased by Brownhills of Nottingham. The SunTor name was revived and used on a number of vehicles, including a camper van version of the Marina's successor, the Morris Ital.

TorCars produced around 2000 vehicles in the decade in which they operated, and the factory near Torrington still exists.

Q10. *How many examples of the Peugeot 405 T16 were produced?*

B.   1046

The Peugeot 405 was undeniably a great success story for Peugeot. Introduced in 1987, it continued to be produced in Europe until 1995 and thereafter continued to enjoy a long and distinguished career in other parts of the world, notably Iran.

UK buyers were treated to two performance versions of the 405: the Mi16 and the Mi16 4x4, both of which were well regarded by the public and press. However, the ultimate roadgoing version of the 405 was never officially imported to the UK. That car was the four-wheel drive 405 T16.

Introduced in 1993, the T16 featured a turbocharged 2.0 litre engine that produced 193 bhp, 33 bhp more than the standard Mi16. Moreover the T16 had a trick up its sleeve: its engine was able to run on a higher boost setting for up to 45 seconds at a time.

Armed with this extra boost, power jumped to an impressive 217 bhp, giving it sufficient grunt to accelerate from rest to 60mph in about 7.0 seconds – impressive for a car that weighed over 1.3 tonnes.

Only 1046 T16s were made, so not only it is a great car, it's also a rare one.

12

UNITED STATES OF AMERICA

Q1. Which 1950s American car was built in the UK and sold in the USA as a captive import?

B. Nash Metropolitan

The Nash Metropolitan was definitely not your typical American car of the 1950s.

It was small, frugal and wasn't actually built in the USA. Moreover, it was largely aimed at female drivers.

Conceived by Nash Motor Company as an ideal second car, the Metropolitan was built in Britain and used 1.2 litre and 1.5 litre BMC 'B' series engines for motive power. Offered in both hardtop and soft-top versions, production commenced in 1953, with the first examples going on sale in the USA in March of the following year.

Shortly after its introduction, Nash merged with Hudson to form American Motors Corporation. This led to the Metropolitan being sold both as a Nash and as a Hudson. From the 1958 model year on, however, it was sold simply as a Metropolitan in North America. The Metropolitan was also sold by BMC, both as the Austin Metropolitan and (in New Zealand) as the Nash Metropolitan.

Although the Metropolitan was relatively cheap, it never sold in the sort of numbers that its makers had hoped, and a total of just under 95,000 North American versions had been built when production ended in 1961. Added to that, BMC produced a further 9390 or so examples for sale in other markets.

Q2. *Which US car was popularly known as 'the goat'?*

B.   Pontiac GTO

These days, 'GOAT' is an acronym for 'greatest of all time', but a little under 60 years it referred to the daddy of all muscle cars, the Pontiac GTO. And one of the creators of the GTO was – believe it or not – a certain John Zachary DeLorean.

Having joined Pontiac in 1956, DeLorean had worked his way up to the position of Chief Engineer by 1961. But whilst Pontiac cars sold well, they had a slightly staid image compared to other brands, lacking what we'd now call a halo model. DeLorean was one of those who set about changing that.

The solution that DeLorean and his associates (principally Bill Collins and Russ Gee) hit upon was a simple one – drop a large engine into a small car. The engine chosen was GM's 389 cubic inch (6.4 litre) V8, and the car into which it was to be fitted was the Pontiac Le Mans, one of the smaller cars produced by GM.

First, though, there was a problem to be circumvented. GM policy stated that no engine larger than 330 cubic inches (5.4 litre) was to be fitted as standard to a car of the size of the Le Mans. The way around this was to offer the larger engine as part of a GTO option package. With the backing of Pontiac's General Manager Pete Estes, the project was approved and the GTO became reality.

It became a great success; it sold well and enhanced Pontiac's image. It also boosted DeLorean's career at General Motors, to the extent that in 1965 he became the youngest-ever person to head a Division at General Motors.

As for calling the GTO 'the goat', that was a product of youth culture rather than of its makers. There are various suggestions as to why it attracted that nickname, but the most likely (if least interesting) reason is that it's a simply a corruption of 'GTO'.

Q3. *The Renault 11 was sold in the USA as the Renault...?*

C.   Encore

The fourth-largest car producer in the USA, American Motors Corporation generally lived in the shadows of its larger domestic rivals: Chrysler, Ford and General Motors.

In spite of having produced some successful models (and having the Jeep as part of its product roster), AMC was struggling towards the tail end of the 1970s. It therefore sought a partner who could both invest capital and offer new models to fill the void resulting from AMC's decision to cease production of some of its existing models. That partner was Renault.

By 1982, the French company owned 42% of AMC, making it the largest shareholder. But Renault had to more to offer than just money – it also had new model ranges which could be adapted to meet US legislative requirements.

Thus it came to pass that AMC built US-market versions of the Renault 9 and 11, respectively sold as the Renault Alliance and Renault Encore (which later became known as the Alliance Hatchback). A Renault GTA was also available in the USA, but this was a 2.0 litre version of the Alliance rather than the rear-engined coupé sold in Europe.

Sales were initially brisk but fell away considerably as time passed. Even so, by the time that production ended in 1987, following Chrysler's acquisition of AMC, around 624,000 examples of the Encore and Alliance models had been assembled in North America.

Q4. *Which US company was best known for manufacturing taxi cabs?*

D. Checker

There was a time when the Checker name was virtually synonymous with taxi cabs in the USA. That it did so was largely down to one man: Morris Markin.

A Russian emigre, Markin had arrived in the USA with neither money nor the ability to communicate in English. However, by a process of hard work and sound judgement, he quickly rose to become a successful clothier.

His business interests diversified when he acquired a vehicle body manufacturing company, which he renamed 'Markin Automobile Body'. And when one of his new acquisition's customers, a company named Commonwealth Motors, ran into financial difficulties, Markin acquired it too.

When Markin acquired Commonwealth, it had an order to supply taxi cabs to Checker Taxi, a Chicago-based company. Markin fulfilled this order by supplying cabs from his newly created Checker Cab Manufacturing Company, which he had formed by merging Commonwealth Motors and Marklin Automobile Body. He then went on to acquire both Checker Taxi and the Yellow Cab Company during the 1920s, giving him a ready market for Checker cabs.

The early 1930s were difficult years for US motor manufacturers, including Checker. Markin, too, had something of a turbulent ride, even being voted off the Checker board at one point. However, he was able to regain control, remaining at the helm until his death in 1970.

By the 1970s, however, Checker's designs were very dated. Several proposals for a new, modern Checker cab were mooted, but as the company continued to turn a profit there was little appetite for change. This led ultimately to a situation in which the cost of creating a new Checker cab was deemed to be too great, with the result that Checker ceased to manufacture taxi cabs in 1982. The company did, however, continue to operate until 2009 as a manufacturer of body parts for the likes of GM and Ford – some ten years after the last Checker cab in New York city switched off its meter for good.

Q5. ***Which car was pictured with the Apollo 12 crew in 'Life' magazine?***

B.   Chevrolet Corvette

Thanks to a racing driver named Jim Rathmann, winner of the 1960 Indianapolis 500, the Chevrolet Corvette was the car most closely associated with NASA's Mercury, Gemini and Apollo astronauts.

The association began at the start of the 1960s when Rathmann, who owned a Chevrolet dealership a few miles from the NASA launch facility at Cape Canaveral, became friends with several of the would-be Mercury astronauts, most of whom were lovers of both sports cars and motor sport.

Through that friendship, a programme emerged whereby General Motors leased new cars via Rathmann's dealership to astronauts in return for a nominal annual payment. It made for great – and relatively cheap – publicity at a time when first the Space Race and later the Race to the Moon enthralled the USA.

Many of the astronauts who acquired cars via the lease programme chose General Motors' sportiest car, the Corvette. This included the crew of Apollo 12: Alan Bean, Pete Conrad and Richard Gordon all acquired Corvettes painted gold and black to match the colour of the lower part of their lunar module. Naturally, the three astronauts and their cars were much photographed, including a spread for *Life* magazine.

The crew of Apollo 15 also plumped for Corvettes – a red one, a white one and – you've guessed it – a blue one. They and their cars also appeared in *Life* magazine, pictured with a Lunar Rover. But with Chevrolet ending the lease deal in 1971, that was the beginning of the end for the Corvette as the astronauts' vehicle of choice.

Q6. *The Mitsubishi Starion was marketed in the US by Chrysler, Dodge and Plymouth as the...?*

D. Conquest

In 1970, Chrysler acquired a 15% share in Mitsubishi Motors. This led to several of the Japanese company's cars, which were smaller and more efficient than those produced by Chrysler, being sold in the USA as Dodge, Plymouth and Chrysler models.

The Starion was introduced in 1982 and was introduced to the USA by Mitsubishi in 1983. A year later, Chrysler got in on the action by selling badge-engineered versions of it as the Dodge Conquest and Plymouth Conquest from 1984 to 1986, and as the Chrysler Conquest from 1987 until production ended in 1989.

One car, one market, four names.

Q7. *What was the name of the range of all-wheel drive cars introduced by AMC in 1979?*

A. Eagle

Essentially the brainchild of Roy Lunn, the Chief Design Engineer for Jeep (then owned by AMC), the Eagle turned out to be AMC's last hurrah – a clever and practical range of cars that broke new ground by being the first production car to be equipped with permanent four-wheel drive (although the option to run in two-drive mode was later added).

Launched in 1979, the Eagle was based on AMC's Concord platform, although the Eagle had an additional three inches of ground clearance and, thanks to the weight of its additional drivetrain components, was rather heavier. Like its parent car, it was available in several different body styles: station wagon, saloon, hatchback, and coupé. A soft-top version, converted for AMC by the Griffith Company (owned by the same Jack Griffith whose name appears on certain TVR models), later followed.

Although highly regarded by the motoring press, the Eagle's sales figures failed to match its ability. Its case wasn't helped by its maker's financial difficulties which persisted even after Renault became its largest shareholder.

The Eagle briefly remained in production following AMC's acquisition by Chrysler in August 1987 but production ended before the year was out.

Q8. *In which US State will you find the art installation known as the Cadillac Ranch?*

C. **Texas**

Created in 1974, Cadillac Ranch is an art installation located in Amarillo, Texas. It is composed of ten Cadillac models dating from 1949 to 1963, each of which is buried nose-first in the ground. The juxtaposition of the cars is intended to show the evolution of the tail fins which was a staple element of their styling.

It was created by architects Chip Lord and Doug Michels, and art student Hudson Marquez, all of whom were members of an art group named Ant Farm. Cadillac Ranch was initially located in a cornfield but was moved in 1997 to a cow pasture adjacent to Interstate 40. Both locations belonged to the project's benefactor.

Cadillac Ranch has attracted the attention of writers, film makers and musicians over the years, including Bruce Springsteen, whose song, *Cadillac Ranch*, appeared on his 1980 album *The River* and was released as a single in various countries.

The cars have been repainted in different colour schemes from time to time and have been popular with graffiti artists. In 2019, however, one of the Cadillacs – the oldest of the ten cars – attracted less welcome attention when it sustained damage as a result of arson.

Q9.   *Which of the following US marques was the first to disappear from new car showrooms?*

D.   Packard

Founded in 1928, Plymouth was a part of Chrysler (and its successor, Daimler Chrysler) throughout its lifespan. Best known for its 1950s to 1970s offerings, including the *Fury*, *Barracuda*, and *Valiant* – it was a victim of its parent company's financial troubles, to the extent that most of its later offerings were badge-engineered versions of Dodge and Mitsubishi models.

The marque made a brief return to the limelight in the late 1990s with the retro-styled Prowler but disappeared from showrooms in 2001.

As explained elsewhere in this book, AMC was founded in 1954 but disappeared in 1987 following its acquisition by Chrysler.

Packard was founded in 1899. Although a moderately successful car manufacturer, it is best perhaps best known as a manufacturer of aircraft and marine engines. It famously produced a badge-engineered version of the Rolls Royce Merlin aero engine, which was used to great effect by the P-51D Mustang (which was ironically known as 'the Cadillac of the skies').

In 1954, Packard bought the ailing Studebaker Corporation, and a new company was formed: Studebaker-Packard Corporation. There had been some talk of further mergers with Nash and Hudson but these came to nothing. As it was, Studebaker's financial position was rather worse than Packard had imagined, and Packard's previously strong financial position soon weakened.

This was followed by a raft of other issues, which further chipped away at the corporation's finances. This led to the demise of Packard as a marque in 1959. Studebaker continued for a time, but a strike at its South Bend factory in 1962 further harmed the ailing marque's finances. Production of Studebaker cars in the USA ended in December 1963 but its Canadian facility continued to operate until March 1966, when it too closed its doors.

Q10. ***The EV1 was an electric car produced by which manufacturer?***

B.   General Motors

In some respects, the story of the General Motors EV1 mirrors that of the Citroën M35 and the Chrysler Turbine Car, in that cars were supplied to members of the public for use in a real-world test programme. And like the M35, most of the EV1s were subsequently scrapped by their maker.

Inspired by GM's Impact electric car of 1990, the EV1 relied solely on battery power as a means of propulsion. It was built in two series, the first of 660 cars and the second of 457 examples, and leased to customers in several cities.

There were several key differences between the two generations, with the second series cars being lighter and quieter. Furthermore, later second generation cars were supplied with nickel-metal hydride rather than lead-acid batteries, which gave a useful increase in their range.

As might be expected, there were teething troubles with the EV1, and 450 first generation cars were recalled in 2000 to have a potential fire hazard rectified. That said, feedback was positive, and it came as something as a surprise when GM announced in 2002 that they would not be renewing the leases on the EV1 fleet. They went a step further in 2003, announcing the cancellation of the EV1 project.

Although a number of EV1 drivers sent deposit cheques to GM in the hope of being able to continue to lease their EV1, the company stood firm on its decision to recover each EV1 at the end of its lease. By September, 2004, the entire EV1 fleet had been recovered by GM. They then donated a number of deactivated* EV1s to museums and technical institutions and destroyed the rest.

GM's decision to terminate the EV1 project and destroy the existing cars was criticised by environmental campaigners and was the subject of a 2006 documentary film, *Who Killed the Electric Car?*

*The EV1 donated to the Smithsonian Museum was not deactivated.

13

FIRST AND LAST

Q1. *What was the first production car to feature remote-controlled central locking?*

D. Renault Fuego

Let's start with a simple fact: Renault did not invent remote-control central locking. That particular accolade belongs to a man named Paul Lipschutz.

Lipschutz was an engineer with Neiman, a French company whose founder, Abram Neiman, was born in what was originally part of Russia, became part of Romania and is is now part of Moldova.

Neiman's life story is one of perseverance and eventual triumph in the face of adversity. Having been unable to attend university in Russia because of his Jewish faith*, Neiman moved to France in 1912 in order to study in Toulouse.

Two years later he was interned for four years in Germany as an enemy alien, having been travelling home through Germany to see his parents when war broke out. The experience didn't put him off Germany, as he moved there in 1922 and set up an engineering business. He remained in Germany until 1938, when he fled to France.

Following the defeat of France in 1940, Neiman had to go into hiding until France's eventual liberation by the Allies. Tragically, both of his parents were victims of the Holocaust.

After the war ended, Neiman returned to the engineering business, setting up his own company, Neiman S.A. In the 1950s, he was joined by Paul Lipschutz. Over the years,

Lipschutz came up with a number of innovations, not the least of which was a system whereby vehicle doors could be locked and unlocked using a small infrared transmitter within a keyfob.

Lipschutz filed for a patent in 1979, and the system was ready for mass production by 1980, whereupon it was offered to vehicle manufacturers.

Renault was the first to bite, fitting the system to higher-specification versions of its Fuego coupé from late 1982. Taking its name from an abbreviation of its inventor's first and last names, 'Plip' remote central locking was a great success, quickly being introduced on other models throughout the Renault range and beyond.

*At the time, Russia imposed a limit on the number of Jewish people who could study at university – an example of what is known as *numerus clausus*.

Q2. *What was the last Alfa Romeo to enter production before the company became part of Fiat?*

A. 75

Like many car manufacturers, state-owned Alfa Romeo found itself in financial difficulties in the 1970s. This was due to a combination of factors including high inflation, industrial unrest and low productivity, particularly at the Pomigliano d'Arco factory built to produce the Alfausd.

In 1980, agreement on a joint venture between Alfa Romeo and Nissan was reached, and a new factory near Naples was constructed. It was here that the progeny of the alliance, the Alfa Romeo Arna – essentially a combination of a Nissan bodyshell and (mostly) Alfa Romeo running gear – was assembled. Unfortunately, the Arna was a flop, with the result that the Italian government sought a fresh suitor for the embattled company.

Fiat initially proposed the setting up of a joint venture with Alfa

Romeo, but this offer became a takeover bid after Ford expressed an interest in acquiring part-ownership of Alfa. Fiat's bid was accepted, and in 1986 Alfa Romeo became part of Fiat's then burgeoning empire.

One consequence of this was that the Alfa Romeo 75 saloon, introduced in 1985, has the distinction of being the last Alfa Romeo to go into production before Fiat's takeover. It wasn't, however, the last Alfa to be developed in the pre-Fiat era – that accolade goes to the 164 saloon which entered production in 1987.

Q3. *In what year did the first mass-produced Ford to have front-wheel drive go into production?*

B. 1962

The first front-wheel drive Ford was the third generation of the West German-built Taunus, which was launched in 1962.

Known to some as the Taunus P4, its origins lay not in West Germany but in the USA, where it was originally intended to go into production as the Ford Cardinal. Following a change of plans, the project (which was at a very advanced stage) was switched from Detroit to Cologne.

Larger and more comfortable than its chief rival, the Volkswagen Beetle, the Taunus P4 suffered from a number of niggling problems and never came close to challenging the Beetle's position as the most popular new car in West Germany.

When production of the Taunus P4 ended in 1966, it was replaced by the slightly larger Taunus P6, which retained its predecessor's front-wheel drive layout. However, it too failed to achieve the desired sales level, with the result that Ford switched back to a simpler rear-wheel drive layout for its successor. Indeed, it wasn't until the advent of the Mondeo in 1992 that Ford reverted to a front-wheel drive configuration for its large family car.

Q4. *In what year did Nissan cease to use the Datsun brand name in the UK?*
A. 1984

In 1931, the Japanese car manufacturer DAT Automobile Manufacturing chose to name their new small car 'Datson'. This name was continued, and indeed became a brand name, following DAT's absorption into the Nissan Motor Company. There was, however, one change: as the word 'son' can mean 'loss' in Japanese, it was quickly replaced with 'sun'. And thus Datson became Datsun.

Nissan's road cars were branded as Datsuns until the 1960s. One reason for this is that Nissan had manufactured trucks for the Japanese military, and in the aftermath of World War 2 there was a desire not to associate the company's road cars with its military vehicles.

In the UK, the Datsun name was supplanted by Nissan in 1984, although it would take a further two years for it to disappear from all global markets.

Q5. *In which production car did rally ace Tony Pond lap the Isle of Man TT circuit at an average speed of over 100 mph?*
C. Rover 827 Vitesse

Tony Pond was no stranger to success on the Isle of Man, having won the Manx Rally on four occasions between 1978 and 1986, so it was perhaps inevitable that he would become the first man to lap the full TT course at an average speed of over 100 mph in a production car.

Pond's first attempt came in 1988 at the wheel of a Rover 827 Vitesse, the idea being that the publicity which would result from a successful attempt would boost the image of the newly-launched 800 series. The 827 used by Pond was effectively a standard car, save for its roll cage, rally-spec seats, tyres and exhaust.

Unfortunately, the course was damp in places, and this caused Pond to narrowly miss his target.

He and the Vitesse returned in 1990, and this time he was able to achieve the 100 mph mark. Given the size and weight of the car, and the fact that it drove only its front wheels, it was a magnificent achievement.

Pond's lap was recorded by an in-car camera and is currently available on DVD or to download from Duke Video. I can't recommend it highly enough.

Q6. *In what year was 'Motor' magazine absorbed into 'Autocar'?*

D. 1988

In 1902, a new weekly motoring magazine was launched in the UK. Entitled Motorcycling and Motoring, its name was changed to The Motor in 1903. It kept that name until 1964, when it was shortened to simply Motor.

Like its chief rival, *Autocar*, *Motor* contained a diet of news and feature articles, product reviews and detailed reports on road tests carried out by the magazine's staff. It was noted for the high quality of its journalism and was home to a number of highly-regarded motoring journalists such as Roger Bell, Tony Dron, Michael Bowler, Hamish Cardno, Rex Greenslade and Jeremy Walton.

The last issue of *Motor* as a separate entity was dated 31st August 1988. It was thereafter absorbed into *Autocar*, which was published as *Autocar & Motor* until reverting to *Autocar* with effect from 21st September, 1994.

Q7. *Whose company was the first to offer a V8-engined version of the MGB?*

A. Ken Costello

MG's first attempt to produce a more powerful version of the MGB effectively foundered on the rock it carried up front – the 2.9 litre, six-cylinder Morris C-series engine was both heavy and somewhat disinclined to rev, as buyers of the MGC soon discovered.

BL had another, altogether more suitable engine in its armoury, the 3.5 litre Rover V8, but it took the efforts of another company to show them the way. The story goes that Ken Costello - an engineer who was no slouch as a racing driver, having won the 1967 BRSCC Redex Gold Cross Saloon Car Championship in his 1.3 litre Mini Cooper S - saw a demounted Rover V8 engine in a friend's workshop and realised that it was both light and compact enough to make an ideal power unit for the MGB. He therefore decided to create a V8-powered MGB.

Two years elapsed between Costello starting work on the first V8-powered MGB in 1969 and the completion of the first production example. The result was an impressively quick and well-engineered car that showcased both Costello's talents and the MGB's potential.

At BL's request, Costello took one of his V8-powered MGBs to Abingdon, sufficiently impressing BL's top brass for them to instruct that BL should produce its own MGB V8. Costello was not, however, invited to participate in that project. Moreover, BL thereafter made it difficult for him to acquire the engines he needed. And that, coupled with the 1970s energy crisis, effectively brought series production of the Costello MGB V8s to an end after around 225 had been produced.

Q8. What was the last Citroën car to be introduced with an air-cooled engine?

A. Axel

In 1948, the Citroën 2CV became the marque's first car to be powered by an air-cooled engine – a diminutive, two-cylinder unit with horizontally opposed cylinders. It was simple, rugged and reliable.

It was joined in 1970 by a larger air-cooled unit, this one having twice the number of cylinders but retaining the smaller engine's horizontally-opposed configuration. It debuted in the GS and, like its older two-cylinder sibling, saw service in several other vehicles, including the Starck AS-37 biplane.

Of the two, it was the two-cylinder unit that continued in production the longer, due to the longevity of the 2CV. However, it was the four-cylinder unit which powered the final new Citroën to be released with an-cooled engine option in its range.

Although this car, the Citroen Axel, was launched in 1984, it had its roots in a car from the previous decade: *Prototype Y*. Intended to slot into the Citroën range between the 2CV and the GS, *Prototype Y* was shelved when Peugeot took over Citroën. The project was subsequently sold to the Romanian company Oltcit, in which Citroen held a minority stake. On going into production in 1982, both its two-cylinder air-cooled engine and gearbox were supplied by Citroën.

It became a Citroën in 1984, when it was imported to France and sold as the Citroën Axel. However, in spite of a very attractive price policy the Axel was not a hit with buyers, and only 60,184 had been built when production of it* ended in 1987.

Although not a model revered by marque enthusiasts, the Axel was not only the last Citroën model to be introduced with an air-cooled engine but also the last Citroën to be designed before Peugeot took over the company.

* By which I mean production of it as a Citroën. It continued to be sold in Romania in various guises until 1996, five years after Citroen had withdrawn from its Romanian joint venture.

Q9. *The prancing horse seen on Ferrari's logo was originally used by...?*

C. Count Francesco Baracca, a WW1 fighter ace

Ferrari's logo features three elements: green, white and red bands to represent the flag of Italy, the yellow of Modena, and the most distinctive part of the logo, a black prancing horse.

The prancing horse (il cavallino rampante, as it's known in Italy) was originally the personal emblem of Count Francesco Baracca, an Italian fighter ace who was killed in June 1918.

There was no personal connection between Enzo Ferrari and Francesco Baracca, but several years after the war ended Ferrari, who was then a racing driver with Alfa Romeo, met Baracca's mother*. The upshot was that she asked Ferrari to use the logo on his racing car.

As used by Ferrari the driver and, later, Ferrari the constructor, the horse differs in several respects from that used by Baracca. Apart from stylistic differences, Ferrari chose to have a black horse rather than the red one used by Baracca.

*Accounts vary as to the location and circumstances of this meeting.

Q10. *What make of car was on board RMS Titanic when she made her ill-fated maiden voyage?*

C.   Renault

The RMS Titanic was carrying a single car in her hold on her maiden voyage in 1912, a Renault CB Coupe de Ville. Like the ship that carried it, the Renault (which produced 35 bhp from its 2.6 litre engine) was built for comfort at the expense of outright speed.

Perhaps it was this quality that attracted the attention of William Carter, a wealthy American who was on an extended holiday with his family in Europe. Carter purchased the Renault and arranged for it to accompany his family and their household staff across the Atlantic Ocean to the USA. It was thus placed into one of the ship's forward cargo holds at Southampton.

Carter became separated from his wife and children in the chaos that ensued after the ship's fatal encounter with an iceberg. However, his wife, children and the family maid all escaped the sinking ship on a lifeboat and were later picked up by the Carpathia.

Carter also survived, having followed J. Bruce Ismay, the chairman of the White Star Line, into one of the last lifeboats launched before the Titanic foundered. Alas, neither Carter's manservant nor chauffeur were fortunate enough to find a seat in a lifeboat, and both perished on that cold April night.

No photographs survive of Carter's Renault but a non-functional replica of a 1912 Renault was made for the 1997 film, *Titanic*. The cost of this replica no doubt comfortably exceeded the $5000 claimed by Carter for the loss of his car.

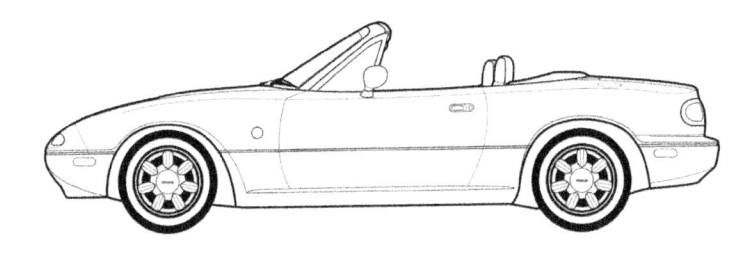

ABOUT THE AUTHORS

David M. Milloy (writer)

David practised law for over twenty years before escaping from the legal profession in order to fulfil a childhood ambition by becoming a motoring writer.

Since changing career, David has written for a number of publications in both printed and digital media, including *Classic Car Weekly*, *Complete Kit Car*, *Absolute Lotus*, and *Influx*.

This is David's fith book. His previous books – *The Ultimate Unofficial F1 Quiz Book*, *The Ultimate Classic Car Quiz Book*, *Lesser Spotted Classics*, and *The Lost Highway* (a collection of short fictional stories with a supernatural bent) – are all available from Amazon. David is also the co-host, with James Ruppert, of the Bangers and Classics podcast:

www.losthighway.online

Russell Wallis (illustrator)

Russell has been a self employed automotive illustrator and graphic designer for the last 12 years. He has worked with clients on personalised car illustrations designed books for self publishers and much more in between.

He has been interested in cars his whole life, which evolved into a desire to become an automotive designer and illustrator. He spent four years at Coventry University studying automotive design, where he developed his illustrative and graphic design skills.

Russell has a created large portfolio of classic automotive art over the last 12 years, which can be found on his website together with links to his online stores.

www.rjwcreativedesign.co.uk

ALSO BY THE SAME AUTHOR

Paperback:

The Ultimate Unofficial F1 Quiz Book

The Ultimate Classic Car Quiz Book

Lesser Spotted Classics
21 Great cars you (probably) won't see on the road
(with Russell Wallis)

Kindle Ebook:

The Ultimate Unofficial F1 Quiz Book
(with illustrations by Marcus Ward)

The Lost Highway
(fiction)

Printed in Great Britain
by Amazon